Beating Mediocrity

Beating Mediocrity

Six Habits of
the Highly Effective Christian

John Guest

Foreword by
Joseph M. Stowell

BAKER BOOK HOUSE
Grand Rapids, Michigan 49516

To
my dear friends and co-laborers
in the evangelistic ministry—
Clare and Susan DeGraaf
and their children,
Jennifer, Molly, Megan, Betsy, and Tyler

Contents

Foreword

The word mediocre is hardly a compliment. It describes that vast lethargic middle territory of existence where words like "average," "OK," "not real bad, not real good," "fair," and "it'll do" reside. While no one ever aspires to mediocrity, it just happens when we choose to avoid that which is clearly bad, without aspiring to that which is powerful, positive, effective, and significant.

In terms of our walk with Christ, a discussion of mediocrity should be irrelevant except for the fact that so many of us who belong to this community of Christ live out our faith in such mediocre ways. Tragically, mediocre Christians produce a mediocre church and discount the reality of an excellent God.

It's out of my desire that the church of Christ make a strategic and significant impact that I'm delighted to recommend this book by John Guest to your mind, heart, and life. He sketches for us six habits that take us beyond mediocrity to an effective and empowered expression of our Christian faith.

John's clear and succinct treatment of habits like Bible study, prayer, engaging in worship, sharing the faith, enjoying fellowship, and practicing giving, will cultivate the soil of our hearts to bring forth the kind of righteousness that will deliver us from the comfortable yet sterile confines of mediocrity.

This book provides a great way to introduce new believers to the elements of following Christ. Local churches will find this an effective tool for training God's people to carry out the elements of their faith. For the rest of us who have somehow slumped down in this swamp of mediocrity, it will lift us up and take us a step beyond that we may be enabled to live lives that are reflective of the worthy excellence of the One who does all things well.

Joseph M. Stowell
President
Moody Bible Institute

Introduction

I gave my life to Jesus Christ at a Billy Graham crusade in London more than thirty years ago. I went forward to stand at the front. With my eyes closed, I looked into the face of Jesus and thanked him for forgiving me of my sins. I thanked him for coming into my life, for indwelling me. Now I was alive in him—alive forevermore! Heaven was my home, and God was now my Father. But I couldn't know the adventure of growth and learning that lay ahead of me any more than I know what will happen tomorrow, next week, or next year.

Maybe you are a brand-new Christian; this is the first time you have ever really surrendered your heart to Christ. Or maybe you have known the Lord Jesus for many years but recognize a need to pursue knowing him with greater fervor and discipline; you have rededicated or recommitted your life to the Lord. No matter how long you have known the Lord, the six habits of the effective Christian are the ones we will discuss in this book: Bible study, prayer, worship, witness, fellowship, and the use of your money.

No one wants to be known as mediocre, just as no one wants an average marriage or a modest job. Deep down, where the ambition of our soul lies, we want to be all that we can be. We dream of excelling and making an impact on the lives and circumstances of those around us. When all is said and done, we want to know we really made a difference.

This book is for Christians who want to excel for Jesus Christ. It is for the young Christian who wants to get ahead quickly in his or her pursuit of Christian excellence. Similarly, it responds to the newfound desire of the recommitted Christian, who doesn't want to "slip slide" back into mediocrity. New enthusiastic church members will find in these chapters a way to contribute significantly to the life of their church family. This is a book about how to "go for it!" and not come back. But first, I want to encourage you to stand firm on the foundation of the Christian gospel. So we will begin by reviewing the heart of the Christian faith and the confidence that is ours because we belong to the Lord Jesus.

1

The Menu of Faith

For God so loved the world that he gave his only
Son, that whoever believes in him should not
perish but have eternal life.

(John 3:16)

Have you ever watched a little child—curious, constantly in motion, every waking moment an invitation to adventure and unexplored opportunities? Children exemplify
the human instinct and desire for knowledge. Every one of
us must go through a period of not knowing; it's a normal
step in the process of education. We don't come ready-made
with all knowledge; we need to quest after it. Sadly enough,
life's experiences have deadened in so many of us the quest-
ing, searching spirit of our childhood. But it is precisely that
search Jesus promises to reward:

Ask, and it will be given you; seek, and you will find; knock,
and it will be opened to you. For every one who asks receives, and he who seeks finds, and to him who knocks it
will be opened. (Matt. 7:7–8)

This process cannot be short-circuited. Nor can it be
stereotyped. Each of us must tell our own story—for some,
it is short and simple, for others long and tortuous. But one
thing is sure: virtually everyone who comes to a living faith

13

in Jesus Christ passes through various stages of unbelief. The most common first reaction on meeting a verbal Christian—one who talks about his faith—is antagonism. Often it's a friend who has gone through the struggles already and unloads with great enthusiasm what God has done for him. You can hardly believe it! Your friendship is jeopardized; and you are not sure how to relate from there on. I have seen tremendous strain put on marriages when a husband or wife begins to talk this way.

In the second phase, you gather information because Christianity poses a growing threat to your cherished attitudes and life-style. Perhaps this book was put into your hands by a friend. Perhaps as part of your search you picked it up at a bookstore. But it represents to you this ambivalent phase of finding out more of what Christians believe. And yet all the while you are terribly threatened and put off.

The third phase is a growing desire to find for yourself what your Christian friends seem to have discovered. You are almost thoroughly convinced that what they say has intellectual integrity, but more than that, the quality of life these Christians and "their friends" exhibit has become extremely attractive to you. You have pretty much resolved your ambivalence and are positively searching for a way to make an entrance into this new world of faith and spiritual life.

The Basic Menu of Faith

For many people, having come to this point is rather like standing in front of a great smorgasbord of excellent food and wondering where to begin. Let me share with you the basic "menu" of the Christian faith and perhaps save you some of the frustration of walking up and down the cafeteria counter in confusion.

The first thing to do right now is to stop and pray. Wherever you are right now, be quiet in your own heart and see yourself speaking to God.

Dear heavenly Father,
   I have come to believe that you are the Almighty God who is present here with me now. Even as I pray to you I sense the temptation to step back and return to my doubts and reservations. I ask you to help me give my attention to what you have convinced me is the only way to live a fulfilled and joyful life. Help me to turn my back on the negative attitudes which have dominated my thinking for far too long, and turn to face you. Please grant that I may know the life-giving truth of your Son, Jesus Christ. Amen.

You may need to dwell on this prayer for a while. Make it a real conversation with God, and see yourself in private audience with him, being as open and honest in your heart toward him as you know how.

As we proceed, you may need further explanation in one or more of the following areas of truth. We each come with a different awareness of need, with different struggles in our search for peace with God. For this reason I will spell out clearly each "course of the menu" so that nothing essential will be missed.

First of all let me set the outline before you.

The Character of God
   His Holiness
   His Love
The Plight of Humankind
   Sinful
   Alienated
What God Has Done
   The Death of Christ
What We Must Do
   The Gift of Believing

The Commitment of Faith
It's Our Choice

The Character of God—Holiness

Personal communication

We begin by recognizing that there are two personages involved when God communicates to us: God himself who initiates the communication, and we who must respond. It is this very situation, God being who he is and we being who we are, that colors his communication to us. Put another way, God is multifaceted in his personhood, just as we are. He is not monochromatic in his character and identity any more than we are. But because of who we are as needy human beings, there are two aspects of God's revealed character which have an immediate impact on us: his awe-inspiring purity and his overwhelming love.

Some biblical examples

In the Bible, whenever people were confronted by the living God, the first thing which seized their hearts was his utter holiness. For instance, Moses, to whom God revealed himself in a desert wilderness "in a flame of fire" (Exod. 3:2), heard these words, "Do not come near; put off your shoes from your feet, for the place on which you are standing is holy ground" (Exod. 3:5). What was Moses' response? To hide "his face, for he was afraid to look at God" (Exod. 3:6).

Read also verses one through five of Isaiah chapter 6:

> In the year that King Uzziah died I saw the Lord sitting upon a throne, high and lifted up; and his train filled the temple. Above him stood the seraphim; each had six wings: with two he covered his face, and with two he covered his feet, and with two he flew. And one called to another and said: "Holy, holy, holy is the LORD of hosts; the whole earth is full of his glory." And the foundations of the thresholds shook at the

voice of him who called, and the house was filled with smoke. And I said: "Woe is me! For I am lost; for I am a man of unclean lips, and I dwell in the midst of a people of unclean lips; for my eyes have seen the King, the LORD of hosts!"

Notice how in the presence of God the seraphim, which literally means "burning ones," hide their faces and their feet from the presence of the living God. Hear their reverberating calls of worship, "Holy, holy, holy is the LORD of hosts; the whole earth is full of his glory." And hear Isaiah's cry, "Woe is me! For I am lost."

On the road to Damascus, Saul of Tarsus met the risen Lord Jesus in the form of a blinding light (see Acts 9:3–8). The Bible sums it up this way, "God is light and in him is no darkness at all" (1 John 1:5).

What holiness means

In simple straightforward terms, God's holiness means three things.

First, it means *God is morally perfect.* He is in himself the expression of all perfection. His commandments are not arbitrary, as if he could change them at whim. He can't change the rules of the game because we messed them all up and wouldn't play right. He is not like the lawmakers who, because the vast majority of people flout a given law, simply change it to accommodate their behavior and thereby protect the integrity of the law.

Nor does God grade on the curve. He doesn't take the median of human behavior and use it as the standard by which he will judge everyone. He does not have a book called *Situation Ethics* in his library.

Right is right and wrong is wrong, not primarily because God says so, but because of who he is and what he is like. It is because of what God is like that he says what he says. The world is not a vast Monopoly game he has designed, making up rules just so there can be winners and losers.

His expressed standards for the way we should live spring from his very nature—who he is.

Second, it means *God is perfectly just.* Not only is his standard perfection but he weighs and judges all things perfectly. His perceptions are not errant. He does not make poor "judgment calls." There is no weakness that makes him respond out of defensiveness, or threat to his identity that causes him to act with rashness. He cannot be bribed. He is "no respecter of persons." There is not the slightest hint that, like our court system, there is one judgment for the rich and another for the poor. There are no legal technicalities which can ever divert the course of justice. All of us can count on absolute and impartial justice at his hand.

Third, it means that *sin cannot coexist with God.* God is utterly and altogether pure, and nothing corrupt, warped, or sinful can coexist in the rare climate of his presence. Just as certain organisms cannot live in the light of the sun, neither can sinful men and women in the brightness of his holiness.

Holiness versus evil

Many can bear witness to the chilling fear of the presence of evil. Nightmares are a universal experience. But how many have been awestruck by holiness? Have you ever wondered about the fascination with horror movies? When did you last see a film that tried to capture the nature of holiness? There are many authors who can paralyze us with the fear and horror of evil. Can you name an author who has inspired you with his portrayal of holiness?

The truth is that we know plenty about evil because it is everywhere present. We know very little about holiness until God in his mercy begins to show himself to us. Perhaps it is that we can handle the horror of evil better than the sheer intimidation of holiness.

And yet sooner or later there is an aching in the heart for the beauty of holiness, the desire "to be pure as he is pure." The original image in which we were created, that of the living God, still lingers as a distant memory and longing. We have inherited vestiges of what God meant us to be, and by them, deep reaches out to deep to bring us to himself.

The Character of God—Love

Love is the second and overwhelming side of God's character. God said to his chosen people, Israel, "I have loved you with an everlasting love." The author who said, "God is light," also says, "God is love" (1 John 1:5; 4:8). Perhaps the most famous verse of the Bible is the one which begins, "God so loved the world . . . " (John 3:16).

It is the love of God that reaches out in mercy. "There is forgiveness with thee," says Psalm 130:4; and in Daniel 9 we read, "To the Lord our God belong mercy and forgiveness" (v.9). In the Bible the single most constant expression of God's love is his desire to forgive and the lengths to which he has gone that we might be forgiven. His "steadfast love" is nearly always expressed in terms of his offer of forgiveness.

The dilemma of love and justice

These two characteristics, God's holiness and God's forgiveness, seem to be incompatible. On the one hand the holiness of God drives us away in judgment, but on the other hand his mercy bids us come and be forgiven. If God is just, how can he be merciful? If he is merciful, how can he be just? It appears that if he is to be just he must close off his mercy, and if he is to be merciful he must deny his justice. We will return to this dilemma in a moment, but first we must consider one other problem.

The Plight of Humankind—Sinful

We miss the mark

In the light of whom God has revealed himself to be, we now review the character of humankind. The reason we are so threatened by the holiness of God is that we are sinful. After a muddy game of football, a player may not feel out of place alongside all the other muddy players, but take him immediately from the field of play and present him at the head table of a formal banquet, and he will feel extremely conspicuous. Similarly, one man judged alongside another may feel perfectly content, but in the presence of the God we have just described he only wants to get away as soon as possible. And when there is no place to which he can run, then all he can do is hide his face.

We are sinful

The Bible says, "All have sinned and fall short of the glory of God" (Rom. 3:23). Sin, then, is not just seen in the odious terms of murder, rape, or robbery, but in terms of falling short of God's glory. The English word *sin* has its origin in the ancient sport of archery. When the archer was shooting long distances at a target, a man would call and tell him if he had missed or not. When he missed, the call to the archer was "sin." You have missed the mark.

The Bible also tells us that we are "all sinners." We have all missed the mark. "None is righteous, no, not one" (Rom. 3:10). That is, not one of us is perfect the way God is perfect.

The personal reality of sin

Perhaps this is not startling to you. To most people it is self-evident. Hardly a door is made without a lock in it. We have not lived up to our own limited standards, let alone God's. Not one of us would like our secret thoughts made public. If all our friends were gathered at a movie theater, and suddenly, by some genius of scientific technology, it was announced that everything we had ever thought about them was now to be shown on the screen, we would be the first to leave. No doubt we would not have a friend left after the showing!

The gravity of sin

It is not difficult to come to terms with our being sinners. What *is* difficult is coming to terms with sin's gravity; the Bible makes it plain that "the wages of sin is death" (Rom. 6:23)—not physical death, but spiritual death. To people who had come to new life in Christ, Paul wrote, "You he made alive, when you were *dead* through the trespasses and sins" (Eph. 2:1, italics added). We can understand a little better the problem of this "death" to God when we think a moment of how physical death affects us.

Physical death is an affront and indignation to our human sensibilities. We hate to be in the presence of death and are repulsed by it. I have seen men angry at the knowledge of their own imminent death—men who all their lives had everything under control and could buy whatever changes they wanted to effect. Death was an invasion of their self-determinism and their dignity.

This is but a small indication of the affront and indignation that spiritual death is to the living God. This is one of the reasons that the Jew, having touched a dead person or animal, was excluded from worship until he or she had gone through certain rites of cleansing. It was an outward and visible teaching of how abhorrent spiritual death was to God. The statement, "Your iniquities have made a separation between you and your God" (Isa. 59:2) is more than a separation as by a wall or by distance; it is the separation of death.

The Plight of Humankind—Alienation

We are estranged from God

So it is that we are, by nature, alienated from God. Spiritually dead men and women, of necessity, live in a state of alienation from God. Again, hear how the Bible describes it, "They are darkened in their understanding, alienated from the life of God because of the ignorance that is in them, due to their hardness of heart" (Eph. 4:18). Writing to those who had once been in such a state, the apostle Paul said that they were at one time "estranged and hostile in mind" (Col. 1:21).

We long for intimacy with God

We need to recognize immediately that God did not create men and women to live in this state of spiritual death and alienation. Just as there is a haunting longing for the purity of God, so we want to escape from the loneliness that comes with our estrangement from God. Like salmon returning to their place of birth to spawn, we innately yearn for the life and fulfillment for which God created us.

We may try many substitutes on our way to discovering the life that God alone can give. We may look to love, marriage, and family for care and intimacy. We may pursue career advancement for wealth, power, and identity. We may throw ourselves into leisure and pleasure to find happiness. We may invest in the worlds of learning and the arts for creative stimulation and expression. We may sacrifice our body's appetites to be healthy and live long. We may enter the rigors of religious discipline.

In the song "Eleanor Rigby," John Lennon poignantly wrote about lonely people, wondering where they all come from and where they belong. It is a reminder that nothing can ever take the place of God. As Pascal said, "There is a God-shaped vacuum in every life." Augustine said, "We are restless until we find our peace in God."

What God Has Done

We have seen in concise straightforward terms that the living God revealed himself to be extreme in his holiness and yet extraordinary in his love. This particularly touches our human awareness because of our human plight—we are sinful, and our sin means spiritual death and alienation. We inwardly long for reconciliation. It is precisely at this point that we must turn to the earlier dilemma we posed—God's seemingly irreconcilable justice and mercy. We, on the one hand, are helpless to change our own condition, and it appears that God, on the other hand, must deny an essential part of his character whichever response he makes.

Resolving the dilemma

The marvelous news of the Christian gospel is that God has solved this problem in the person of his Son Jesus Christ. For in Christ, God has come among us and done for us what we could never do for ourselves. He has borne the judgment we deserved and expressed the reconciling love of God which we needed. Once again we turn to what the Bible teaches:

> Therefore, if any one is in Christ, he is a new creation; the old has passed away, behold, the new has come. All this is from God, who through Christ reconciled us to himself and gave us the ministry of reconciliation; that is, in Christ God was reconciling the world to himself, not counting their trespasses against them, and entrusting to us the message of reconciliation. So we are ambassadors for Christ, God making his appeal through us. We beseech you on behalf of Christ, be reconciled to God. For our sake he made him to be sin who knew no sin, so that in him we might become the righteousness of God. (2 Cor. 5:17–21)

In terms of our discussion let me summarize the main points of this teaching.

1. Christ has taken our place and borne the judgment we deserved (v. 21), so justice is done for the crime committed.
2. Our alienation is done away with by God's reconciling love in Jesus Christ (v. 19), so we are no longer enemies but intimates of God.

3. When we are joined to Christ we become as new creations and are able therefore to stand blameless before a holy God (v. 17).
4. The two sides of God's character which appeared to annul one another, his justice and his love, are both perfectly expressed and fulfilled in the one act of Jesus Christ dying on the cross.

Let me illustrate by taking you to a situation of which I once heard. In a little Tibetan kingdom, the ruler had established by decree that anyone found guilty of robbery would receive thirty-nine lashes. One day his mother was brought before him, caught in the act of stealing. Everyone knew two things: one, if he sentenced her to the punishment it would kill her, and two, if he let her off, his whole system of justice would be jeopardized. The people present waited to see which path he would choose.

He passed sentence—thirty-nine lashes—then stepped from behind his bench of justice and took the punishment himself. In the same way, when God in Christ stepped down from the courts of heaven and died on the cross, God was being both just and merciful. Justice was done for the crimes committed; mercy was extended in that God bore the penalty himself, so that we might be forgiven.

What We Must Do

Exercise faith

There is a necessary response on our part to the initiative God has taken. Nothing is automatic. God has purchased a valuable gift for us, but we must receive it. The means whereby we lay hands on forgiveness and the gift of eternal life is *faith*. "Believe in the Lord Jesus, and you will be saved" (Acts 16:31).

Since faith is a very difficult concept for many people to grasp, let's spend a little more time looking at it. It is important to know how to respond properly to God's amazing offer of love.

Faith is inherent in God's character

To begin with, I have often asked myself why God has chosen to make faith the means of not only receiving his love and forgiveness, but also the means by which we continue to live in relationship to himself. I have drawn the conclusion that faith is not an arbitrary scheme invented by God, but part of God's very existence, and it expresses the nature of his being.

It is not the purpose of this book to delve into the triune personhood of God—Father, Son, Holy Spirit. But suffice it to say that within the "one Godhead" are three persons, and before God ever created humankind, his own existence was lived out in mutual interpersonal fidelity or faith. The Bible teaches that even when we are "unfaithful," God remains faithful. "He cannot deny himself" (2 Tim. 2:13). The characteristic of God's nature is *faithfulness*. As God has revealed himself in the recorded history of the Bible, he did it as a God who makes covenants or trust agreements. Deuteronomy 7:9 says he "keeps covenant." That is, he remains steadfastly faithful to his pledge or promise.

Faith is inherent in human character

When God created human beings, he did so saying, "Let us make man in our image, after our likeness" (Gen. 1:26). The nature of our existence then, created as it is in the image of God, has the potential and impetus to exercise faith. Our fundamental relationships cannot exist without trust. Husbands and wives make a faith commitment to each other in the sacred pledge of marriage. Parents and children, friends and associates, thrive on trustworthiness. It is the common coinage of all human transactions. Fidelity always affirms personhood, and infidelity always diminishes it.

When looked at in a broader light, faith sets free tremendous creative energy. We are inspired to bring into reality "things which are not." It is exciting to see men and women accomplish great things through the exercise of faith—not in God necessarily, but just as an expression of human creativity and entrepreneurial vision.

The athlete who has faith in his ability is the one who surpasses even his own imagination. When parents exhibit faith in their children they spark achievement beyond expectation. A manager's faith in those he leads can inspire them to produce outstanding results. It is faith which transforms problems into opportunities and dreams into realities. Faith lifts human existence above the mundane and perfunctory, bringing creative challenge and exuberance. Faith is indeed "the assurance of things hoped for, the conviction of things not seen," and "by it the men of old received divine approval" (Heb. 11:1–2).

Faith in Jesus Christ

How, in specific terms, does the Bible speak about believing in Jesus Christ?

> He was in the world, and the world was made through him, yet the world knew him not. He came to his own home, and his own people received him not. But to all who received him, who believed in his name, he gave power to become children of God; who were born, not of blood nor of the will of the flesh nor of the will of man, but of God. (John 1:10–13)

A similar and graphic image is projected in Revelation 3:20: "Behold, I stand at the door and knock; if any one hears my voice and opens the door, I will come in to him and eat with him, and he with me."

Believing is receiving

Faith is described in terms of "receiving Christ." Note that *receiving* and *believing* are used to describe a response to the Lord Jesus and that each word in turn qualifies the other. To believe is to receive, and to receive is to believe. Unbelief, by the same token, is understood in terms of rejecting Jesus, or of not "receiving" him.

It is very important to see that *belief* is not mere intellectual agreement about Jesus. It is receiving him, embracing him, surrendering to him, depending on him. It is welcoming him into your life to fill the household of your existence.

Believing is choosing

There are many who understand clearly the claims of Christ but have never taken the step of yielding their lives to him. So while in one sense they may say they believe, they have never done anything about it. What they understand in their heads, they do not receive in their hearts. It has been said that the longest eighteen inches in the world is from the head to the heart. Faith, then, is something that has to do with the *will*. Faith is not just intellectually accepting that certain information is true, but it is *choosing* to put our trust and confidence in that truth.

We can see this more clearly if we look at the three parts which constitute human personality. There is the *mind* with which we think; there are the *emotions* with which we feel; and there is the *will* with which we choose.

I know people who have an immense amount of knowledge about Christ but have never chosen to yield their lives to him. I have friends in the ordained ministry who have shared with me that even after their theological education was completed and they were ordained as professional ministers, they did not have a personal relationship with God. For all their formal knowledge about God at the time of their ordination, and even for several years into their ministry, they had not come to that place in their personal experience of putting their faith in him. They knew about God, but they did not know him personally.

Similarly, I know some who have had remarkable religious experiences and have been deeply moved emotionally, but they have never chosen to put their whole dependence in Christ. A perfect example of this is Lord Kenneth Clark, about whom an article was written in *Christianity Today.*

> Lord Clark has just published the second volume of his autobiography entitled *The Other Half: A Self-Portrait.* Sir Kenneth Clark (as he then was) became a household name around the world in connection with the highly successful television series, *Civilization.*
>
> There is an arresting passage in his autobiography in which he writes, "I had a religious experience. It took place in the Church of San Lorenzo, but did not seem to be connected with the harmonious beauty of the architecture. I can only say that for a few minutes my whole being was irradiated by a kind of heavenly joy, far more intense than anything I had known before. This state of mind lasted for several minutes, and wonderful though it was, posed an awkward problem in terms of action. My life was far from blameless: I would have to reform. My family would think I was going mad, and perhaps after all, it was a delusion for I was in every way unworthy of receiving such a flood of grace. Gradually the effect wore off and I made no effort to retain it. I think I was right: I was too deeply embedded in the world to change course." (Stuart Barton Babbage, "Lord Kenneth Clark's Encounter with the Motions of Grace," June 8, 1979)

Many people I know would have equated this religious experience with faith and conversion. Lord Clark saw the need for a decision and chose not to believe—that is, chose not to yield his life to the God who had granted the experience.

Christian faith is choosing Christ. Christian faith is receiving Christ. This is why Christians are called by the name *Christ-ian*. The focus of their existence is Jesus Christ.

Believing is possessing

Faith, then, is the means by which God, being who he is, has made it possible for us to *receive* the gift of eternal life. "For this is the will of my Father, that every one who sees the Son and believes in him should have eternal life; and I will raise him up at the last day" (John 6:40). "Truly, truly, I say to you, he who believes has eternal life" (John 6:47).

So it follows that when we place our faith in Jesus Christ, we *have* the gift of eternal life. It becomes a *present* possession. It is not something we wait for and may or may not merit at the end of our lives. When we by faith receive Christ into our lives we receive with him the gift of eternal life. He is "the life" (John 14:6). He said he has come that we might have life in all its fullness (see John 10:10). "He who has the Son has life; he who has not the Son of God has not life" (1 John 5:12).

A gift that is not merited

Two other things become very plain in the light of this teaching. The first is that forgiveness and eternal life cannot be earned or paid for by us. Granted, we do not deserve this extravagant gift of God. To feel unworthy is perfectly normal. Something would be wrong if we felt otherwise. But neither can we do anything to deserve it. A gift is a gift. It is not a reward or a wage. It is a gift which we have done absolutely nothing to deserve. The hymn that captures this so beautifully is "Rock of Ages, Cleft for Me."

Rock of Ages, cleft for me,
Let me hide myself in thee;

Let the water and the blood,
From thy wounded side which flowed
Be of sin the double cure,
Save from wrath and make me pure.

Not the labors of my hands
Could fulfill the law's demands;
These for sin could not atone;
Thou must save, and thou alone;
In my hand no price I bring,
Simply to thy cross I cling.

While I draw this fleeting breath,
When my eyes shall close in death,
When I rise to worlds unknown,
And behold thee on thy throne,
Rock of Ages, cleft for me,
Let me hide myself in thee. Amen.

Secondly, when we receive Christ into our lives, it is to make him the Lord of our lives. When Christ knocks at the door of our lives and we ask him to come in, it is not to stand in the hallway or sit in the kitchen. He comes in to transform the whole household with his presence and leadership. Every room becomes his; the "house" becomes the temple of his Holy Spirit (1 Cor. 3:16).

Faith means changing our life-styles

This then, by direct implication, means we must turn our backs on all that he rejects. The word the Bible uses is *repent*. We don't ask Christ to come and live in a heart that is still determined to oppose him and have its own way. We have to agree with Christ's way.

Further, it means that we must turn from all our sins which put him on the cross. We cannot seek his forgiveness with the clear intention of carrying on as before. When we trust in Christ, we turn with remorse from all that put him on the cross and resolve to live to please him.

It would be very easy for you to misunderstand me at this point. I am not even hinting that you cannot ask Christ into your life until you have put the "house" straight. Christ is the one who cleans us up and makes us new. But we do have to be sorry for all we have done wrong and determine in our hearts that we want to live differently—to live his way.

Faith brings the power to change

Nor am I suggesting that you have to be sure that you are able to live a perfect life and never let Christ down from the moment of your commitment to him. It is the spirit of Christ in you that is going to produce a Christlike life-style.

> Abide in me, and I in you. As the branch cannot bear fruit by itself, unless it abides in the vine, neither can you, unless you abide in me. I am the vine, you are the branches. He who abides in me, and I in him, he it is that bears much fruit, for apart from me you can do nothing. (John 15:4–5)

It is his power and not our determination which makes the difference. What I am saying is that we have to be willing to have him do so and want it to be that way.

So it is through faith in Jesus Christ, who died for us on the cross, that God gives to us forgiveness. It is through faith in the living Lord Jesus Christ that he enters in to our broken human personhood and fills us with his life. It is through faith in Jesus Christ that God has chosen to make us "a new creation."

The Commitment of Faith

We come to the moment of choice. It is possible for you by prayer to choose Christ this very day, and in so doing be made a brand new person. "The old has passed away, behold, the new has come" (2 Cor. 5:17).

Maybe you don't remember ever praying a prayer of commitment. Before we go on, settle it for yourself. Let me lead you in prayer. If possible, find a place to be private where you can kneel down. See yourself kneeling before Jesus Christ. As you drop your eyes to his feet you see the marks of his love. As you lift your eyes to look at his face, you see him looking down at you, loving you as much as the day he died for you on the cross. Then say this prayer aloud, speaking to him:

Dear Lord Jesus,

Thank you for loving me. Thank you for dying for me. Thank you for paying the penalty for my sins. Thank you for offering me this chance to be forgiven and to be made brand new. I give myself to you.

Forgive me all that is past. I am deeply sorry for all the wrong I have done. I want my life to be filled with your power so that I can begin again, made clean and new by you.

Come into my life, Lord Jesus. Come in today, come in to stay. Fill me with your presence. Drive out all the darkness of my old way of life. Confirm in me now the assurance that I am forgiven, that I am made new, that I belong to you.

Thank you for this new beginning. Thank you that you will never leave me nor forsake me. Thank you that wherever I go, and no matter what happens, I am yours and you live in me. Thank you, Lord Jesus. Amen.

You may want to dwell for awhile in the quiet presence of the Lord Jesus, reflecting on the significance of this moment. Look again at John 6:47: "Truly, truly, I say to you, he who believes has eternal life." Jesus, in those words, says to you that if you have believed in him, you *have* eternal life. Similarly, "he who *has* the Son *has* life" (1 John 5:12, italics added). Continue to thank the Lord Jesus that he has given you eternal life; that your home is in heaven;

that your life belongs to him, and that he has a purpose for you.

In being "born again" you have been born into a new family, the family of all believers. You have a new family in Christ. In that family there are all kinds of opportunities to grow more like Jesus Christ and to serve him. Continue to thank the Lord for the new life that is before you.

2

The Search for Certainty

So we know and believe the love God has for us.
God is love, and he who abides in love abides in
God, and God abides in him. In this is love perfected with us, that we may have confidence for
the day of judgment, because as he is so are we
in this world. There is no fear in love, but perfect love casts out fear. For fear has to do with
punishment, and he who fears is not perfected
in love. We love, because he first loved us.

(1 John 4:16–19)

Today we are living in an age of uncertainty. We have
lost our foundation. We no longer know what we believe (if
we believe in anything), or why we believe. It's no wonder
our values are eroding.

In the church there is a well-meaning diffidence that bor-
ders on agnosticism. It is almost as if we have made virtue
out of uncertainty. You often hear people say (either directly
or by inference) that it is arrogant to be certain of what you
believe. Some say outright that you are guilty of the "sin of
presumption" if you *know* you are going to heaven.

Are you struggling with what to believe for yourself so

that you can direct your daily life with a measure of assurance? Then this chapter is for you.

I want to share the "birthright" that belongs to every Christian. It is *confidence;* confidence that we are loved by God personally; confidence that he indwells us personally; confidence that he will never let us go; confidence that he holds us in the hollow of his hand; confidence that we have a destiny in this life; confidence that our home is in heaven; confidence that we can share with others, with our friends and family. In short, it is this very confidence that God intended for his people that transforms the meanest and most ordinary detail of daily life and makes it full of purpose and significance in the grand context of eternity.

A Biblical Certainty

The New Testament makes it plain that we can be certain about our personal destiny. Jesus said,

> I am the good shepherd; I know my own and my own know me . . . My sheep hear my voice, and I know them, and they follow me; and I give them eternal life, and they shall never perish, and no one shall snatch them out of my hand. (John 10:14, 27–28)

The apostle Paul put it this way:

> What then shall we say to this? If God is for us, who is against us? He who did not spare his own Son but gave him up for us all, will he not also give us all things with him? . . . Who shall separate us from the love of Christ? Shall tribulation, or distress, or persecution, or famine, or nakedness, or peril, or sword? . . . For I am sure that neither death, nor life, nor angels, nor principalities, nor things present, nor things to come, nor powers, nor height, nor depth, nor anything else in all creation, will be able to separate us from the love of God in Christ Jesus our Lord. (Rom. 8:31–32, 35, 38–39)

Here is how the apostle Peter explained it:

Blessed be the God and Father of our Lord Jesus Christ! By his great mercy we have been born anew to a living hope through the resurrection of Jesus Christ from the dead, and to an inheritance which is imperishable, undefiled, and unfading, kept in heaven for you, who by God's power are guarded through faith for a salvation ready to be revealed in the last time. (1 Peter 1:3–5)

And listen to the apostle John:

And this is the testimony, that God gave us eternal life, and this life is in his Son. He who has the Son has life; he who has not the Son of God has not life. I write this to you who believe in the name of the Son of God, that you may know that you have eternal life. (1 John 5:11–13)

The reason I quote at length from the Lord himself, two of the eyewitnesses, and Paul is so that you may not be in the slightest doubt about the New Testament teaching. The quotation from Romans is read at every Christian burial in the world almost without exception. It is one of the appointed passages in the Episcopal *Book of Common Prayer.*

Contemporary Uncertainty

What a stark contrast is exhibited between New Testament Christianity and the tepid insecurity which passes for Christian faith today! Suppose the early Christians had sounded like us. Suppose the apostles had spoken like many of our present-day preachers. Suppose, and here I take the liberty of putting modern jargon in their mouths, they had said, "Far be it from me to lay my trip on you." And, "I'm not trying to be dogmatic because I know everyone has his own point of view." Or, "I don't want to put anyone else down, even by implication. I know you're entitled to do your

thing just as I'm entitled to do mine." And the clincher—
"But you never know, perhaps Jesus Christ really had something; perhaps he was even God in the flesh. Maybe he even
rose from the dead. Now don't get me wrong, I'm not wanting to come off as a fundamentalist, and the last thing I want
to do is lay on you a Christianity that is narrow and literal.
But, well, it's up to you. So long as you keep coming to
church and trying to be good you can't go wrong!"

If the early Christians had made statements like these,
do you really think there would be any such thing as Christianity today? Who would have followed them? How could
you commit to such wishy-washy nonsense? It is absolutely
certain that if they had spoken in such insipid noncommittal terms there would be no church today.

One of the reasons membership in the mainline churches
is shrinking—worse still, attendance—is the poverty of the
pulpit. In the diocese of Pittsburgh, for instance, it was re-
ported by the Long-Range Planning Commission of the diocese in 1977, that the viability of close to forty percent of
the parishes was "questionable" or "extremely doubtful."
Pittsburgh, I hasten to mention, is one of the healthier dio-
ceses in the U. S.

Courageous Christians

Where are the Christians of days gone by who had spiritual courage and earthy guts? I'd like to share with you a
few examples. In England, Bishops Nicholas Ridley and
Hugh Latimer were sentenced to death for their faith. On
October 16, 1555, as they were led to the stake, Latimer said,

> Be of good comfort Master Ridley, and play the man. We
> shall this day light such a candle by God's grace in England,
> as (I trust) shall never be put out. (*The Oxford Dictionary
> of Quotations, Second Edition*, Oxford University Press,
> 1953)

Just five months later, on March 21, 1556, Archbishop Cranmer, "the architect" of the *Book of Common Prayer*, died in the same way on the same spot. Earlier in his dispute with Queen Mary and the Roman church he had signed a recantation (a denial of his biblical faith) "for fear of death" as he said. But he went back on that recantation and publicly denied it and as a result was led to the stake. A cross set in the road at Broad Street, Oxford, marks the site. As the flames leapt up around him, he reached down with his right hand, saying that the hand that had denied Christ should burn first.

These stand in a long line of courageous Christians. It is said that there have been more Christian martyrs in this century than in all other centuries put together. Africa and China alone account for most of them. It only stands to reason that martyrs, ancient and modern, knew what they believed. And, if we say we are Christians, we are their spiritual heirs. If not for the courage of the apostles and martyrs we would not be believers today. As Justin Martyr said, "The blood of the martyrs is the seed of the church."

It may seem that I'm advocating martyrdom, but that's not my point. What I am pointing out to you is Christian confidence. These men and women were sure of what they believed. It was a certainty. Note again the Romans passage just quoted. "I am certain nothing can separate us from the love of God in Christ" is their uniform witness. No one could snatch them from the hand of Jesus: he had said so. If you have the Son "you have eternal life," said John. He wrote to those early Christians, "that you may know that you have eternal life." No wishy-washy, I-hope-against-hope kind of attitude here. That confidence can be ours. Individuals are crying out for it in their hearts, and the church is desperate for it in the pulpit.

God Wants Us to Know

When you think about it and are not just swept along by the well-meaning diffidence of the day, one thing becomes crystal clear: God wants us to be sure! If God really loves us would he not want us to know it? Love does not flourish in a vacuum of isolation. Love desires personal fulfillment. I am not just speaking of sexual love. It is true of any love for a parent or child or friend. Fulfillment is seen in terms of a personal relationship and a deep sense of personal sharing with another. This cannot take place if one party is uncertain of the other or doesn't even know the other.

It may sound as if I am suggesting a conditional love where God loves in order to be loved. That is not so. The very nature of love is to seek reciprocation. Put another way, if God were totally indifferent to our response, it would be a clear indication that he didn't really love us. Love cannot be indifferent to the response of the one loved.

It therefore follows that if God loves us he will make it known in personal terms. We don't want to reduce his love to a kind of heavenly handout. Nor, worse still, do we want to attribute to God the kind of misdirected parental love of which we are all very much aware, namely just giving his children "things." As our children need us more than they need things, so we need God more than we need a handout. Of course love means taking care of ordinary practical needs, but God being personal and we being persons, his love would extend beyond the practical to the personal and intimate.

Uncertainty Is Destructive

Uncertainty is, of necessity, destructive of love. I have counseled with men, women, and young people who are uncertain of being loved. Uncertainty breeds insecurity, and insecurity breeds distrust. You can't love a person you don't trust. That is the meaning of the Bible verse, "Perfect love casts out fear" (1 John 4:18). Let's look at the context of this verse:

> So we know and believe the love God has for us. God is love, and he who abides in love abides in God, and God abides in him. In this is love perfected with us, that we may have confidence for the day of judgment, because as he is so are we in this world. There is no fear in love, but perfect love casts out fear. For fear has to do with punishment, and he who fears is not perfected in love. We love, because he first loved us. (1 John 4:16–19)

Note the word *confidence*. What is the basis of such confidence? Knowledge of God's love.

So you see, those who in the name of humility and modesty promote uncertainty are badly misrepresenting God and do you no favor at all. They may as well suggest that your husband can't be trusted, and in the same breath, tell you to love him and serve him and maybe things will turn out all right. What would be wickedly painful is if the husband could have been trusted all along and someone destroyed the relationship by planting a seed of doubt. I have seen exactly that circumstance in a marriage. I have also witnessed it continually in matters of our spiritual life. Don't let anyone ever convince you that God's way is a precarious tightrope of insecurity. The Scriptures assure us, "If God is for us, who is against us?" (Rom. 8:31).

God Wants Us to Be Certain

Perhaps the coup de grace is the expense to which God has gone in reaching out to us. It makes absolutely no sense for God to have given "his only begotten Son" and not want us to know. The very point of the giving was that we might *know*. It wasn't a gesture or token to satisfy himself or the heavenly onlookers. Nor was it a public relations ploy, which is often the case with much public and Christian char-

ity. God did not just want to appear good and extravagant
on our account. He really came to "seek and to save the
lost" (Luke 19:10). Put in personal terms, if God loved me,
and Jesus Christ died for me that I might be forgiven and
made new in Christ, would he not most certainly want me
to be sure to experience all he desired for me?

The extraordinary byproducts of this "blessed assurance"
are joy and freedom; joy wells up in grateful praise and freedom to love back in grateful response. Again, take the example of human love. When the wife knows she is loved
she is able to love freely in return; and, oh, the joy of it!
Gone is the crippling and inhibiting insecurity of, "Do you
really love me?" A child that grows up in the sure knowledge of parental love is free to develop a wholesome and
creative climate of security. So it is in the spiritual realm.

Confident Christians are transformed and transforming.
Marriages are transformed, careers are transformed,
churches are transformed, the future is transformed, for
pessimism is not a Christian virtue. Optimism is. Christian
assurance dispels the one and stimulates the other. Just this
change alone would free many a soul from depression. Without Christ there is much about which to be depressed. Depression is a perfectly healthy response to a hopelessly de-
pressing situation. But convinced Christians see things
through the eyes of Christ. "Through him who loved us,"
says the Bible, "we are more than conquerors" (Rom. 8:37).

I know one lovely young lady who was forced to drop
out of college because of depression. She was for some time
on medication prescribed by a psychiatrist. Her future
looked very bleak—until she met Jesus Christ and became
convinced of his love and forgiveness and his good purpose
for her life. There followed a period of personal growth and
affirmation in the fellowship of the church, and she returned
to college on a scholarship as a voice major.

Another young woman I know came back to her home
town divorced, with two children, a failure in marriage and

with no hope for the future. She came to newness of life in Christ. She shared it with her ex-husband on his weekend visits with the children. Via a different set of circumstances than his ex-wife, he also became a convinced Christian (though her changed life played no small part among the several other influences). After a period of growth in this new life, they remarried—in church on Sunday morning as a witness to the whole community of the transforming power of God's love. He became an ordained minister in the Episcopal church, and they have two more children, twin girls, for good measure.

Isn't this the kind of transformation we want to see in our society? Just imagine our churches full of people meeting in the sure confidence of God's love, a love that has transformed their lives and made them agents of transformation in the lives of others. Imagine preaching that springs from an overwhelming assurance that the God of the Bible is the God of today, and that his promises of love and reconciliation have not changed one iota.

3

One: Use the Manual

All scripture is inspired by God and profitable
for teaching, for reproof, for correction, and for
training in righteousness, that the man of God
may be complete, equipped for every good work.

(2 Tim. 3:16–17)

There is no question that the best-selling book of all time
is the Bible. Most people who know anything about the
Bible have an opinion about it. Many people will tell you
that the Bible is full of contradictions. Others will shrug the
Scriptures off as old legends not to be believed. Others will
say that because they are filled with outrageous stories of
miracles, the Scriptures can't possibly be true.

But what is often the case, those who say it's full of contradictions are rarely able to cite one. Those who say the
Bible is merely a compilation of old legends can never tell
you in what year the Gospel of Mark or the Gospel of John
became legendary writings. Most people do believe in miracles, but they might call them by another name, such as
"extrasensory" or "paranormal."

I have a friend who attended a terrible seminary where
he was instructed, among other things, that you can't trust
Scripture as the authoritative Word of God. Sadly, he came
to believe what he was taught. His wife had believed the

Bible to be true, but after a long period of time, he convinced her that it was not. Then after he was ordained and
ministering in a church, he came to know Christ—the real,
living Christ. It transformed his view of the Bible. But you
know what? He had a terrible time trying to convince his
wife that the Bible *was* the Word of God. Obviously, they
could have avoided the whole problem by searching the
Scriptures to begin with.

As growing Christians, the most important view of the
Scriptures is found in what the Bible says about itself.

New Authority for Daily Living

The verses at the beginning of this chapter, 2 Timothy
3:16–17, are a good place to begin. The Bible is talking about
itself:

> All scripture is inspired by God and profitable for teaching,
> for reproof, for correction, and for training in righteous-
> ness, that the man of God may be complete, equipped for
> every good work.

When you take on a new life in Jesus Christ, you need a
new authority for that life. Your old life had plenty of authorities—maybe even ones you're embarrassed to think
about now. Whether you acknowledge it or not, we all live
under many kinds of authorities.

Worldly authorities

On a recent trip, a gentleman with an enormous newspaper boarded the plane with me. As we flew, he worked
his way slowly through what looked like ten pounds of
newspaper. He never glanced at me, even sideways. There
are many men and women who get up and read the newspaper daily, like clockwork. Of course, it's great to be informed about the world around us, but for many of them,
it becomes a dominant authority in their lives.

For young people, rock music can be an authority. They admire the people who perform the music, so they listen to what the stars say. Rock becomes an authority in their lives.

For some people, a professor at school whom they really admire becomes an authority. Parents are authorities for their little children. Employers are authorities on the current philosophy of doing your own thing, or a desire for pleasure or security or power.

We all have them

But whatever your authorities are, you *do* have them. They are the things that determine how you spend your time and money. All day long, as you make decisions, you're acting on what is most important to you, on your set of beliefs. And behind those beliefs are your authorities.

A couple of years ago I bought a car. It was brand new, with practically zero mileage. The first thing the salesman did was give me the handbook that went with my car and said, "Read it!" Inside the front cover of that book, I read the first words: "Read this book cover to cover." The authority was the manual. If I wanted that car to run well, if I wanted to drive it right and enjoy it for its lifetime, I had to acknowledge and use the authority of its manual.

When we receive a new life in Christ, we come under a new authority. We must yield our lives to the Word of God.

Paul, writing to Timothy, begins with, "All scripture is inspired by God." In the Greek, that word *inspired* literally means "God-breathed." So Scripture is inspired of God, or breathed from God's mouth.

The Bible claims for itself *the authority of God.* So when you yield to the authority of Scripture, you yield to God's authority.

The Church did not give the Bible its authority. If it did, that would make the Church the ultimate authority. Intellectuals who have studied it cover to cover can teach "with authority," but the authority of the Scriptures comes from above—from God, who "breathed" them.

What Is Jesus' Opinion?

The Old Testament

When Jesus lived here on earth as a man, there was no New Testament. It was written later. The New Testament is made up of the Gospels, which chronicle his life and ministry, and the writings of the apostles, those he left behind to carry on his teachings and ministry.

So what is Jesus talking about whenever he refers to God's Word? The Old Testament. The Old Testament was an authority in Jesus' life, and he used it to deal with temptation.

There were two great temptations in Jesus' life—one right at the beginning of his ministry, the other at the end of it.

Matthew 4 tells about the famous temptation of Jesus when he was led by the Spirit into the wilderness and Satan came to tempt him. How did he do it? By saying, "If you are the Son of God, command these stones to become loaves of bread" (v. 3).

And Jesus answered, using Scripture: "It is written, 'Man shall not live by bread alone, but by every word that proceeds from the mouth of God.'" The natural question we want to ask is, "Where is it written?" Jesus is quoting Deuteronomy 8:3. When Jesus was tempted, he quoted the Bible. He went directly to his authority.

Satan tempts him twice more, and Jesus doesn't hesitate. He immediately quotes the Scriptures as a defense against Satan's temptations.

The second great temptation that Jesus faced was at the end of his ministry, just before he went to the cross. Jesus went to the Garden of Gethsemane to pray, "My Father, if it be possible, let this cup pass from me" (Matt. 26:39). He was tempted in that prayer to ask God if there was some other way humankind might be rescued from their lost condition without his sacrificial death. But the second part of that verse shows that Jesus was willing to obey: "Nevertheless, not my will, but as thou wilt." In that great hour of trial when Jesus looked ahead to his suffering on the cross, when he would bear—not just physically but also spiritually—the sin of the world, Jesus asked God if there was another way.

But Jesus was aware of his purpose here and was committed to obey his Father. He used Scripture to demonstrate to his people that he was the Messiah, the long-awaited fulfillment of the prophecies of the Old Testament. In Matthew 5:17–18, he makes it clear:

> Think not that I have come to abolish the law and the prophets; I have come not to abolish them, but to fulfil them. For truly, I say to you, till heaven and earth pass away, not an iota, not a dot, will pass from the law until all is accomplished.

The King James Version says, "One jot or one tittle shall in no wise pass from the law, till all be fulfilled." The jot is the smallest "mark" in Hebrew writing, and the tittle was a tiny decorative curve on the consonants.

Jesus *knew* the Scriptures—the Old Testament—intimately and understood that he was to fulfill it perfectly. So, for instance, after his death and resurrection, the Lord Jesus conversed with two of his disciples without their realizing who he was at first (Luke 24:13–17). They shared their deep distress about the painful events of the previous weekend (Luke 24:20–24). Jesus' response was to teach them about "himself" from the *Scriptures*, "beginning at Moses and all the prophets" (Luke 24:27). But note how emphatic the resurrected Lord was in making his point: "Ought not Christ to have suffered these things . . . ?" he asks them (Luke

24:26). That is, given the Bible's prophetic teaching about the Messiah, his suffering was "inevitable" (J. B. PHILLIPS).

When Jesus wrestled all night in the Garden of Gethsemane and prayed, "Not my will but thine," he knew the will of the Father from the Word of the Father, the Bible. What he taught them after his resurrection was only what he had been trying to impress on them before his suffering and death.

> And taking the twelve, he said to them, "Behold, we are going up to Jerusalem, and everything that is written of the Son of man by the prophets will be accomplished. For he will be delivered to the Gentiles, and will be mocked and shamefully treated and spit upon, they will scourge him and kill him, and on the third day he will rise." (Luke 18:31–33)

Again, the Lord Jesus says, " . . . everything that is written of the Son of man by the *prophets* [in the Old Testament] will be accomplished."

As painful as it was for Jesus, and as much as he (and we with him) might have desired that the salvation of sinful humanity might be accomplished some other way than the cross, the Lord Jesus still surrendered himself to the authority of the Father's will—his Word. For Jesus, the Word of God in the Old Testament was not just a "religious theory" but something he must yield to in the most painful experiential moment of his life.

The New Testament

Now let's turn our attention to the New Testament. I mentioned before that the New Testament is made up of the story of Jesus' life and his words, as well as the teaching that followed his life on earth. Jesus knew that his teaching would be recorded and remembered. The Gospels are full of the words and deeds of the Lord Jesus. In Matthew 24:35 Jesus says, "Heaven and earth will pass away, but my words will not pass away." In Matthew 5:17–18 he clearly demonstrates his understanding of the authority of the Old Testament; now he claims a similar authority for his own words. They will " . . . not pass away."

The Gospels are the writings we call the New Testament, recorded by the apostles—the first disciples of Jesus. Jesus said that under the inspiration and leadership of the Holy Spirit they would pass on those "words which will not pass away."

> I have yet many things to say to you, but you cannot bear them now. When the Spirit of truth comes, he will guide you into all the truth; for he will not speak on his own authority, but whatever he hears he will speak, and he will declare to you the things that are to come. He will glorify me, for he will take what is mine and declare it to you. All that the Father has is mine; therefore I said that he will take what is mine and declare it to you. (John 16:12–15)

Jesus reaffirms his divine authority in this passage: "All that the Father has is mine." And Jesus tells his followers that the Spirit will guide them into all the truth. The Spirit will make known to them what Jesus gives him. What is Jesus saying? That the Spirit under the authority of Jesus "will guide you into all the truth."

Further, the Lord Jesus promised that everything he had taught them while he was with them, that same Holy Spirit would bring back to their memory:

> These things I have spoken to you, while I am still with you. But the Counselor, the Holy Spirit, whom the Father will send in my name, he will teach you all things, and *bring to your remembrance* all that I have said to you. (John 14:25–26, italics added).

So whether it is the Gospel's recording of what the Lord Jesus "began to do and teach" (Acts 1:1), or the balance of the apostles' teaching in the rest of the New Testament, Jesus is the one who inspired it all by sending the Holy Spirit (who in turn inspired the apostles) to accomplish this task.

These verses explain the confidence with which the apostles taught. For example, Peter, Paul, James, and John are not the authorities, although we have been studying their words. Instead it is Jesus who is the ultimate authority, the source of the apostles' teachings. What was the Lord's opinion of the Bible? In his teaching, Jesus clearly understood the authority of the Old Testament, and gave his divine authority to the Gospels and the apostolic teaching of the New Testament.

A New Mind

2 Timothy 3:16–17 says, "All scripture is inspired by God and profitable for teaching, for reproof, for correction, and for training in righteousness, that the man of God may be complete, equipped for every good work." In this verse, Paul gives a twofold reason why God inspired the Word: first, that we might *think right*, and second, that we might *do right*. "Profitable for teaching, for reproof, and for correction," falls into the "think right" category. And "training in righteousness" and "equipped for every good work" is the "do right" section.

There is a definite relationship between these two categories of what we think and how we behave. Most of our behavior is determined by what we think. There is a battle for our minds. Therefore, the mind and how we think is the controlling factor in our behavior, in what we do.

Some people are swayed by newspapers, television, or the last conversation they had. They hear one thing, so they go in that direction. But then they hear something else, so they go in that direction. Their minds become a quagmire. That kind of roving authority leads to the dangerous "if-it-feels-good-do-it" mind-set.

Have you heard this motto: "It's not what you think you are that you are, but what you think, you are"? What you think, *you are*. You *are* the things that fill your mind. The things you think about mold your character. No wonder there is such a battle for the mind!

For growing Christians to celebrate this new life in Christ, they must have the new mind which is in Christ. Paul instructs the Philippians in Philippians 2:5: "Have this mind among yourselves, which is yours in Christ Jesus." Those who have received newness of life can have a new mind. But just how do we go about getting a new mind?

Romans 12:2 tells us: "Do not be conformed to this world but be transformed by the renewal of your mind, that you may prove what is the will of God, what is good and acceptable and perfect." J. B. Phillips paraphrases that verse like this: "Don't let the world squeeze you into its mold." By the renewing of your mind you resist being squeezed into that mold.

One television commercial says, "A mind is a terrible thing to waste." That's true! God has given us tremendous minds, and he wants us to let the Lord Jesus own those minds. He wants us to think like Christ, to see things through the eyes of Christ, to have our worldview become the Christ-view of things.

Now we're back to the difficult question: How do we get the mind of Christ? How can our minds be renewed? The primary way is to give your mind to the Word of authority—the Bible. The Bible is where we learn what God thinks. The Bible is where we discover how God sees things.

This can be a very painful process. When you see things from a human point of view, life is very comfortable. But it can be rather uncomfortable to see things from God's point of view.

Paul had the experience of going to a place and seeing it from God's point of view rather than that of a regular tourist. When Paul arrived in Athens, he took one look at the number of idols everywhere and determined that the Athenians were definitely a very religious people. Acts 17:16 says, "His spirit was provoked within him." Because he knew the truth, it bothered his spirit to see that these people worshiped blindly. While looking at some of the statues and monuments you can still see today in Athens, he even spotted an idol to an "unknown god." Paul was so provoked that he spoke out the truth—the truth about the God who was *unknown* to them but *known* to him. Most of his listeners were not much interested in hearing about Jesus, and the Scriptures say they mocked Paul (v. 32).

Seeing things from God's perspective was uncomfortable for Paul—it provoked his spirit, and he ended up being mocked by the people. And seeing things from God's perspective made the people uncomfortable, too. They didn't want to listen, or they might have to change their life-style. They weren't ready for that.

I believe the number one temptation that keeps us from reading the Bible is that when you get right down to it, it's more comfortable to have the human viewpoint and drift with the crowd than it is to share God's viewpoint and be at odds with the world. Yet, if we desire to renew our minds and have the mind of Christ, we must bring our minds to the Scriptures. The Scriptures have the truth by which we can be informed and then reformed—renewed.

The Right Equipment

We submit our minds to the Word of God not only because we want to think right, but that we might *do* right. Remember 2 Timothy 3:17? The Scriptures make us "complete, equipped for every good work."

I am not a handyman. One of the marks of my not being a handyman is that I don't have the right equipment. Of course, it's very frustrating to try to accomplish a task with the wrong tools. I end up clamping things together with a clamp that wasn't made for the job, or prying things open with a screwdriver that wasn't made for prying. Fortunately for me, my father-in-law is Mr. Handyman, and he brings his tools when he comes to visit so that he can put my house straight before he leaves. Lately he's been leaving the tools at my house so I can try to fix things without him!

But problems crop up when it comes to day-to-day living without the right equipment. We hobble along, botch it up, and dillydally. We are unbelievably inept because we are not thoroughly equipped by the Word of God.

James makes it a challenge: "Be doers of the word, and not [forgetful] hearers only, deceiving yourselves" (James 1:22). We've got to move from thinking and knowing the Word of God to *doing* the Word of God. We can't be forgetful hearers.

That same passage in James goes on to say:

> For if any one is a hearer of the word and not a doer, he is like a man who observes his natural face in a mirror . . . and goes away and at once forgets what he was like. But he who looks into the perfect law, the law of liberty, and perseveres, being no hearer that forgets but a doer that acts, he shall be blessed in his doing. (James 1:23–25)

In the Greek, the contrast is obvious between passive observation and really "looking"—delving into, dwelling upon.

James doesn't want you to approach the Word of God the way you check out your appearance in the store windows as you walk by, just giving a quick glance, then forgetting all about it. He encourages us to absorb the Scriptures so completely that they become an integral part of our lives and spur us to action.

Growing in Glory

We can look to 2 Corinthians 3:18 for encouragement:

And we all, with unveiled face, beholding the glory of the Lord, are being changed into his likeness from one degree of glory to another; for this comes from the Lord who is the Spirit.

When you really look into the Word of God the way James encourages, you are transformed! You become more like Christ. You don't just think like him—you begin to act like him. The reference to glory in that verse is unusual: "changed into his likeness from one degree of glory to another." The word *glory* doesn't mean we start glowing or shining. The translation of that word is *dignity* or *weightiness*. It means we will grow in substance, or with the dignity of God.

In today's society, everyone is looking for dignity. We long for respect; we are offended when people do not treat us with dignity. But our dignity as human beings is derived. It's not inherent. We get it from the Lord, having been created in his image. As we dwell on his Word, look into his Word, and behold him in his Word, we are changed from one glory to another by degrees. We move from our own glory to his glory, from being the world's style of person to God's kind of person.

Jesus closed his teaching in the Sermon on the Mount with this illustration:

> Every one then who hears these words of mine and does them will be like a wise man who built his house upon the rock; and the rain fell, and the floods came, and the winds blew and beat upon that house, but it did not fall, because it had been founded on the rock. And every one who hears these words of mine and does not do them will be like a foolish man who built his house upon the sand; and the rain fell, and the floods came, and the winds blew and beat against that house, and it fell; and great was the fall of it. (Matt. 7:24–27)

There are a lot of collapsing households in our society today. Some people build their personal establishment on love of money; those houses come crashing down with economic adversity. Others build on the quicksand of their careers, their abilities, or popularity. Only the Word of the Lord abides forever. When we build our lives and identity on the Word of God, they stand, no matter what the storm.

It's Nutritious

The Word of God claims to be nutrition. Remember the slogan of the health food fanatics: "You are what you eat"? Jeremiah said, "Thy words were found, and I ate them, and thy words became to me a joy and the delight of my heart" (Jer. 15:16). And Ezekiel had a similar experience:

And he said to me, "Son of man, eat what is offered to you; eat this scroll, and go, speak to the house of Israel." So I opened my mouth, and he gave me the scroll to eat. And he said to me, "Son of man, eat this scroll that I give you and fill your stomach with it." Then I ate it; and it was in my mouth as sweet as honey. (Ezek. 3:1–3)

The collect for the first Sunday in Advent in the 1928 *Book of Common Prayer* reiterates the concept of the Word of God as food:

Almighty God, who has caused all scripture to be written for our learning, grant that we may in such ways, read, mark, learn, and *inwardly digest* it, that by patience and the comfort of the holy Word, we may embrace and ever hold fast the blessed hope of everlasting life, which you have given to us in our Savior, Jesus Christ. Amen. (italics added)

That phrase *inwardly digest* is a clear illustration of how the Word can become nourishment to us.

I confess to you that I am subject to the impact of the mind-set and attitudes of the world around me. Being a pastor or evangelist does not make me exempt. I am not impervious to the world of emotions, thoughts, and actions that touch my life. I've been in such messed-up, awful situations that I couldn't wait to get back to the Word of God to ingest some life and health and nourish my mind on sanity. I need clear, straight teaching. The Word of God brings us into the broad daylight of the truth. With God right is right and wrong is wrong. It is refreshing to leave behind the poison of relativism.

When you're out in the world, you get swept away by the attitudes of people. You begin to wonder what is right today. But not God. He is not up in heaven wondering what on earth is right today. He is the same—yesterday, today, and forever. We need to ingest the mind of the Lord. I love to come back and eat the good food of God's Word.

There's a world of difference between eating junk food and a good solid meal. Sooner or later, we need to recognize the Word of God for the nutrition that it is.

A Powerful Weapon

Second, God's Word is very, very powerful. God spoke through the prophet Isaiah, claiming that his Word will accomplish all that he sends it to do.

> For as the rain and the snow come down from heaven,
>   and return not thither but water the earth,
> making it bring forth and sprout,
>   giving seed to the sower and bread to the eater,
> so shall my word be that goes forth from my mouth;
>   it shall not return to me empty,
> but it shall accomplish that which I purpose,
>   and prosper in the thing for which I sent it.
>   (Isa. 55:10–11)

God's Word is ultimately powerful to accomplish his ends.

God's Word is also described as being very sharp. Ephesians 6:17 calls the Word of God the "sword of the Spirit." Hebrews 4:12 fills out that picture: "For the word of God is living and active, sharper than any two-edged sword, piercing to the division of soul and spirit, of joints and marrow, and discerning the thoughts and intentions of the heart."

So the Scripture claims for itself the power to do what God sends it to do and the sharpness to divide up our human personality like soul from spirit, marrow from bone. Scripture is God's scalpel. It does precision work.

One of the things we discover—and it makes us very uncomfortable—is that when we come to judge the Word of God, we invariably find ourselves being judged by it. The Word of God comes sharply into our lives, and it's very uncomfortable. Sometimes we don't want to hear what it says because it means we must make a change in our habits or attitudes. But we have to admit, God's Word is powerful!

So if you want to have an influence for good and for God in this world, what do you need? You need the powerful weapon of the Word of God in your heart so that you speak with the authority of the Lord. Of course you can't go around like a speaking Bible, but your words will be rooted in the truth of God's Word. You can declare that truth and live that truth, applying it relevantly to a world you understand.

Which Bible?

In terms of reading the Bible, I recommend that you get yourself a modern paraphrase, such as *The Living Bible* or *Good News for Modern Man* or *J. B. Phillips' New Testament*. Paraphrases put the Scriptures into colloquial language. You also need a standard translation, like the King James Version, the Revised Standard Version, the New

American Standard Version, or the New International Version. These are translations, not paraphrases or transliterations. If you get your hands on both, read quickly the colloquial paraphrase to get the general idea. When you actually get down to studying, looking into, beholding God's Word, then use the standard translations.

Making Time

Set a time for yourself to study. If your life is like mine, you are extremely busy and you usually only get done what you plan to do (and maybe not even that!). Plan to spend time reading the Bible. Some people call such a program of personal study a "quiet time." It's your personal quiet time with God.

The Scriptures are like good food. Once you've tasted them, you want more. But you do need to set a time. For all the help and power that the Word may hold, for all that we believe about it, it's not going to do us any good unless we give ourselves to it. Get your hands on it and your mind around it.

Learning to study the Word of God for ourselves is the step that takes us from Christian childhood to Christian adulthood. If you are struggling with this, I encourage you to set aside a time and go for it. When you blow it and miss that appointed time, set aside another time and try again. And when you blow it again, set aside another time and go for it again. Look out—the devil is committed to keeping you from reading the Word of God. So be persistent, even when it isn't easy.

You don't have to defend the Word of God. Martin Luther, the leader of the Reformation, said, "You may as well try to defend a lion. Let it out of the cage and it will take care of itself." Get the Word of God out of the cage of those bookends, and its transforming power will be revealed in your life and in the lives of others.

Making It Practical

Let me give you some useful ideas which will help you in your Bible study.

- Pick a specific time each day (preferably in the morning) and make a covenant with God that this is your time with him. If you have a difficult time keeping awake in the morning, make a cup of coffee or tea. Relax and enjoy God's Word for you.
- Take a minute to ask God to reveal himself to you through his Word, and ask the Holy Spirit to bless this time of study.
- Take time to meditate on a thought or concept which the Holy Spirit will place on your heart.
- When reading, substitute your name in place of the person or persons being spoken to. God *is* speaking to *you*. Underline important verses.
- Invest in an easy-to-understand study Bible and read the author's comments when you do not understand a verse.
- Begin memorizing Bible verses that are important to you and set a goal for memorization. (The Navigators *Bible Memorization System* is excellent.)

    These tips available from "Personal Renewal Month," a program from The John Guest Evangelistic Team, 3366 Burton St. S.E., Grand Rapids, MI 49546.

The following study guides are excellent tools to aid you in your Bible reading (try your local bookstore):
- *Walk Through the Bible*, a yearly Bible study
- *Scripture Union*, a three-year daily reading program
- *Through the Bible in a Year*, a yearly Bible study

4

Two: Cultivate Prayer

For all who are led by the Spirit of God are sons
of God. For you did not receive the spirit of slavery to fall back into fear, but you have received
the spirit of sonship. When we cry, "Abba! Father!" it is the Spirit himself bearing witness with
our spirit that we are children of God.

(Rom. 8:14–16)

The Christian who is committed to grow in the Lord
takes prayer seriously. Since communication is the lifeblood
of any relationship, the ability to communicate with the
Lord of the universe is one of his great gifts to us. The following principles of prayer and suggestions for prayer will
help you make the most of that great gift and will bring you
into a stronger, deeper relationship with God.

Intimacy

The first principle of prayer is that it is *an expression of
intimacy with God.* Prayer is not like dispatching a
telegram or sending a memo through the office. Prayer
comes out of a relationship. The second part of Romans
8:15 describes our relationship to the Father: "You have received the spirit of sonship. When we cry, 'Abba! Father!' it

is the Spirit himself bearing witness with our spirit that we are children of God." *Abba Father.* The word *Abba* is the Jewish way of saying "Daddy." These verses are a holy, warm, intimate description of a child's relationship to God as Father. The apostle Paul claims that when we cry out to God, we cry out, "Daddy!"

Prayer is first of all the expression of our hearts when we cry out to God in intimacy. We are able to say *Daddy.* The Scripture says the reason we have this intimacy is because we have been adopted by the spirit of God into the family of God. Romans 8:14 emphasizes this: "For all who are led by the Spirit of God are sons of God." We are sons or daughters, not slaves.

Verse fifteen follows it up with, "For you did not receive the spirit of slavery to fall back into fear." Our relationship to God is not primarily that of master to slave. Without question, we *are* servants of God. And when we're in the presence of God we are awestruck by his mightiness. But our spirit is not the demeaning, degrading spirit of slavery leading to fear again. When we are born again of the spirit of God, God's spirit comes to indwell us, and we are adopted as spiritual children into the family of God. Those who come to prayer knowing that God is an intimate Father, those who can say *Abba,* are those who have been born again spiritually into God's intimate family.

Granted, there is a sense in which all of us are God's offspring just by being human and part of his creation. In an impersonal way, the whole of creation owes its origins to God because he is the author of all creation. But in the personal and intimate sense of prayer and relationship to God, it is only those who have received Christ into their lives, whom the Holy Spirit has regenerated to newness of life, who know an intimate relationship with God.

There was a time when I didn't know God intimately. In those days it was like shouting up to the heavens to talk to him. I talked to him only when I really needed something—

a job, a career idea, or the assurance that I would pass an exam. As a child I suffered earaches, and I can remember asking God to get rid of them. But for years I did not know God as someone close and personal and caring.

The day I asked Christ into my heart, into my life, our relationship was transformed. The next morning, I awoke and thought, "I am not alone." My first thought used to be, "Where are my cigarettes?" But that morning, the cigarettes were my *second* thought. I walked out of the house that morning knowing that God walked with me.

I was eighteen years old, and adolescent loneliness was a problem. When I came to know God, my loneliness was gone. I walked with him—not because I had been taught to—because as a new Christian I had been taught next to nothing. It just felt natural to talk to him as someone personally very close to me because I had been born again by his spirit into his family. That intimacy is the first principle of prayer.

Talking to God should be personal—like talking to one another. I encourage you to talk out loud when you talk to God, especially when you are alone. Don't just offer him your thoughts, even though your thoughts are in words and sentences in your mind. Intimacy is enriched when you speak those words out loud and hear yourself talking to God with words that you can hear.

It's not enough for husbands and wives to *think* to each other, "I love you." When a husband says to his wife, "I love you," it not only pleases his wife, it pleases him. Similarly, when we relegate prayer to our thought lives alone, it is less personal, less an expression of intimacy than when we pray out loud. I don't advise you to pray aloud as you walk down the street, but at home, in your car, and as often as you can, talk out loud to God. It will make him more intimate and real.

Constancy

The second principle of prayer is *constancy*. Because the prayer relationship is a continuing relationship, we can be constant in it. This relationship is not a fleeting, passing relationship. God never leaves us. He has promised, "I will be with you; I will not fail you or forsake you" (Joshua 1:5), and "I am with you always" (Matt. 28:20). No one can take us out of God's hands. Proverbs 18:24 talks about a "friend who sticks closer than a brother." Jesus is that friend. God has promised his steadfastness, his fidelity to us. Consequently, we can talk to him anytime, all the time.

1 Thessalonians 5:17 says, "Pray without ceasing" (KJV). The Revised Standard Version says, "Pray *constantly*." Paul repeats the injunction in Ephesians 6:18: "Pray at all times in the Spirit, with all prayer and supplication. To that end keep alert with all perseverance, making supplication for all the saints." Constancy is expressed throughout the passage: ongoing commitment to sharing what's going on in our lives, praying at *all* times, staying alert with *all* perseverance for *all* the saints.

Did you know the human brain never stops thinking? Even when we are asleep there is an unconscious cerebration—the mind factors things it has heard, the things that you think about. Have you ever had the experience of pondering a dilemma and then leaving it alone for several days? Then suddenly the light goes on and you see the solution clearly. What has happened? Unconsciously, your mind went on working even though you were not giving conscious awareness to those thoughts.

It's an obvious application to a mind that never rests to give itself to something positive. However, we often use our thoughts negatively. We think about hurts and insults and people who have let us down. Or we think about how we have failed people and begin to denigrate ourselves. Wouldn't it be better just to turn all of that into prayer? Instead of "I failed my husband," pray, "Lord, I don't know if I can ever put that right, but do some work of healing in our relationship." Turn those problems into prayer.

Years ago, my landlady in Bristol, England, had this little motto on the wall in the bathroom: "Why pray when you can worry?" We get addicted to worrying about our failures, limitations, and unsolvable problems of family economics. We worry about the color of the bathroom, which wallpaper to choose, how to make the kids do their homework, whether the boss is happy with our work. We could turn those conscious, waking, worrying moments into practical opportunities for prayer.

As a student, I had the most difficult time with anything that had to do with history. I hated history, so I tried not to bother with it. Unfortunately, that attitude was reflected in my exams! When I became a theological student, I had to learn the history of Christianity; how it influenced, and has been influenced, by the history of the world. And the history of Christianity is not one glorious, fun-filled day—it's murky and sordid. There are parts of Christian history that all Christians are ashamed of, and I had to *memorize* those parts.

I began to talk out loud to God about all those dates and events. I would walk around my room talking to God and say the things in my history book out loud, committing them to memory. Then I would talk to the Lord about what I had just memorized. The walls in our dorm rooms were so thin that the fellow next door to me became concerned for my sanity because he began to hear me talking all the time! But sharing what I was learning with the Lord, while I was learning it, transformed a miserable task into another way of growing in my relationship with Christ.

Make it a habit—the second principle of prayer is *constancy.*

Solitude

The third principle is *solitude*. When the disciples came to Jesus and said, "Lord, teach us to pray," he taught them what we call the Lord's Prayer as a model. The first thing Jesus taught them was to be *alone* with God as an intimate. The first words of the Lord's Prayer are *Our Father*—there is that intimacy again. Then, in the solitude of that reflection, *hallowed be thy name*. Mark 1:35 says, "And in the morning, a great while before day, he rose and went out to a lonely place, and there he prayed." If Jesus got up early in the morning while it was still dark to be alone with God, he had a predetermined commitment to be there. Scripture teaches that it was his habit to get up and go and find that lonely place. It was his habit to seek solitude with God.

When Jesus said, "Truly, I say to you, if you have faith and never doubt, you will . . . say to this mountain, 'Be taken up and cast into the sea,' it will be done," he knew it for a fact! He had spent time alone with God, being quiet with him and sharing events with him, even as life was going on. It seems amazing that right when the news about him was spreading even farther and when even greater multitudes were gathering to hear him and be healed of their sicknesses, he would often slip away into the wilderness to pray (Luke 5:15–16). He didn't say to everybody, "Stop, I am going to pray; wait here for three hours till I get back." He would just slip away very quietly. He needed to be alone with God in the wilderness in the midst of the pressure and busyness.

Hudson Taylor was one of the first missionaries to China who went inland to live as a national. He was so busy he would often say, "The busier I am, the more I need to pray." How different from us! We are so busy, we don't have time to pray. Solitude is becoming a lost ingredient in the human personality. There just isn't time for reflection, time to be alone in God's presence. We have radio alarm clocks, televisions, telephones, stereos in our cars. We fill our lives with clamor.

We need to take our key from the Lord Jesus, who was hounded by the demands of people like none of us have ever been hounded. He didn't even have a room that was his own! Luke 9:58 says, "The Son of man has nowhere to lay his head." He couldn't go into his bedroom, shut the door, and say, "Go away, world." He had to discipline himself to seek out a place of solitude to pray. We have a lot to learn from Jesus' example.

Discipline

The fourth principle of prayer is *discipline*. We've already mentioned that Jesus got up early in the morning while it was still dark. Each of us knows how difficult that is whether we are morning persons or night persons. One of the reasons we in Western civilization have so little solitude with God is that we've got so little discipline.

Discipline has even become a dirty word to us. When we hear the word, we think of spankings, of being rapped over the knuckles by the teacher. But discipline is the only way to freedom. Discipline is the doorway to a creative, alive life with time to do the things that need to be done, especially to pray.

The person without discipline gets nothing done. He's like a farmer who goes to get the eggs but sees the pump leaking across the farmyard, so he stops his trip to the henhouse to get the washer to fix the pump. On his way to get the washer, he sees that the hayloft needs to be straightened. Forgetting the washer, he starts fixing up the hayloft. On the way to get the pitchfork to use in the hayloft, he sees that the broom handle is broken. So he thinks, "I must make a note to get a new broom handle." On his way back to the kitchen to write himself the note, he . . . Well, you get the idea! Nothing ever gets done.

Discipline allows us freedom. For example, some people don't want to learn methods for sharing their faith—they want to be spontaneously led of God. But you know, they actually have no freedom to do so. If you haven't memorized the multiplication tables, you can't be free to do arithmetic without checking your work over and over. But if you have memorized them, you can come up with those numbers spontaneously. If you memorize Scripture references and a pattern for sharing your faith, you'll have what you need there at your fingertips—you'll be free to share your faith. We need a similar discipline in prayer.

A couple of years ago, a friend gave me an autographed edition of Rocky Bleier's biography. Rocky Bleier was number 20 during the great years of the Pittsburgh Steelers. He was injured in Vietnam and the story of his recovery is remarkable. He tells how the first time he tried to run around the track, he fell at the end of one lap, sweating and weeping. When he talked to his doctor about whether he would ever play football again, the doctor told him he would be fortunate if he just learned to walk properly.

On his first Super Bowl Sunday, Rocky's mind flashed to other experiences. He remembered those horrifying weeks when nothing seemed to help—not physical manipulation, not electric shock treatment. His therapists nearly gave up. He remembered a thousand painful mornings when his alarm clock awakened him at five thirty, when it was dark and cold outside. His body ached, and something inside would tell him, "Later. You can skip this morning's workout. Do it later, this afternoon or tonight. Stay in bed." But he kept getting up to run himself to the brink of exhaustion. He says, "Through the whole ordeal I was at peace within myself. My fulfillment strangely, almost masochistically, was in the workouts, in the sweat, in the ache, in conquering the five thirty A.M. temptations." (Rocky Bleier, *Fighting Back*. New York: Stein & Day, 1975, 112–46.)

All that discipline to play football, and today Rocky Bleier's football career is over. But we can learn something from him. Aren't we called to the same commitment and discipline to being alone with God each day before we go into the excessive demands of contemporary life? I believe we are. And you know what? Our careers as Christians will never be over!

Prayer Power

The principles of prayer are intimacy, constancy, solitude, and discipline. There are five components to prayer which can help transform your prayer-life. I've organized them under the first five letters of the alphabet.

Adore

A stands for our need to *adore* the Lord. The temptation is to run into God's presence with a grocery list in the same way we run into the supermarket. We come with our list and say, "Lord, give me this, I want this, give me that, hand me the other. Do this for Harry and Mary and my husband and the kids." It becomes just a litany of need. Have you ever noticed that when you do that, you find yourself dwelling on needs and wants? Instead of talking to God, you end up talking to yourself about the problems rather than praying about them.

I have noticed that when we pray, the devil tempts us insidiously by bringing extraneous things to mind—things that have something to do with the matters we bring to God in prayer. For instance, if you are praying for your children, suddenly you think, "Oh, I must remember to buy Tommy those tennis shoes!" And then you're thinking about the cost, and which store, and when you are going to get it done, etc. . . . Eventually you're not praying anymore.

One way to deal with this problem is to use a notepad when you pray. Instead of being like the distracted farmer mentioned earlier, jot down the thing you've just remembered and then go back to praying. Your mind can rest because you've jotted it down. It turns the diversions into further opportunities for prayer and getting the job done properly!

When the Lord taught the disciples the Lord's Prayer, "Our Father who art in heaven, hallowed be thy name," he was giving priority to being with God in his presence—just loving him! A young mother once said to me, "I can't wait for my baby daughter to wake up. I hate it when she's asleep. I just love to have her awake." Does she love to hear the baby cry and scream and carry on? Of course not. She loves that baby. She wants to look and enjoy and *adore*. That's what we ought to do with God. The Scripture says to "delight" in him (Ps. 37:4). The first condition of prayer is to delight in him, to *adore* him.

Let me give you some useful ideas which will help turn your prayer time into a time of adoration.

- Begin by praising God for a new day!
- Dwell on God's presence in your life and his promises to you.
- Sing hymns and choruses that you have memorized.
- Recall as many names for God and Jesus as you can remember, such as:
    The Lamb
    Counselor
    Creator
    High Priest
    Anointed One
    God Almighty
    Our Shield
    Shepherd
    Redeemer

The Rock
Bread of Life
King of Kings
Turn these names and titles into gratitude and praise.
- Praise him for all the good things in your life.

*These tips available from "Personal Renewal Month,"
a program from The John Guest Evangelistic Team,
3366 Burton St. S.E., Grand Rapids, MI 49546.*

Be bold

The *B* reminds us to be *bold*. Hebrews 4:16 says, "Let us then with confidence draw near to the throne of grace, that we may receive mercy and find grace to help in time of need." Let us draw near with confidence. The King James Version says "with boldness."

The world hesitates to get too close to God. The world is afraid of him. People who don't know intimacy with God, who don't have that relationship to God, even dislike the name of God; they use it as profanity. People who have that attitude don't really love God, and they don't come to him with any confidence. They profane him at a distance. But Christians can come with confidence into his presence. We should not come with hesitancy and timidity, with our heads hung in shame. Rather, we should come with confident anticipation, knowing we are specifically encouraged by God to come. He is more willing to hear than we to pray. He wants us to come, so we come with boldness.

Confess

C is for *confess*—the need to confess our sins. One of the ancient prayers of the Christian church begins, "Almighty God, unto whom all hearts are open, all desires known, and from whom no secrets are hid." What an honest way to bare your heart before God. We are simply admitting and confessing openly before him our need for his mercy and forgiveness because of our sin. Our lives are an open book before him anyway, so why try to hide?

Isaiah 59:2 says, "Your iniquities have made a separation between you and your God, and your sins have hid his face from you so that he does not hear." We need to get the sin out of the way so the lines for holy communication are open. Our forgiveness is forever for all sins, because Christ died once for all our sins. When we come to God, it's not so much that we're groveling and begging him to forgive us, because we know he wants to forgive us. We are simply openly admitting and confessing to him that we are sinners in need of his forgiveness. It's an open way of relating our humility—humility for which we have good cause!

Following World War II, Winston Churchill was succeeded as the prime minister of England by Clement Atlee, who later became Lord Atlee. Winston Churchill was asked, "What do you think of the new prime minister?" He replied, "He is a very modest man who has much about which to be modest." That's a clever put-down!

Although we come boldly into the presence of God, we know there is much about which we have to be modest and even ashamed. Openly acknowledge that before him. 1 John 1:8–9 says, "If we say we have no sin, we deceive ourselves, and the truth is not in us. If we confess our sins, he is faithful and just, and will forgive our sins and cleanse us from all unrighteousness." Humility and truthfulness about our sin before God is an appropriate attitude for maintaining an open relationship with him.

Describe

D is to *describe* any situation, to talk to God about it. We have a tendency to come to him with ready-made solutions and say, "Do this for me, Lord." We make the *D* mean *demand*. God, do this, do that, do the other. We need to scrap that approach and learn to *describe* our petitions to him, talking with him about all the aspects of the problem: "Lord, you know what happened last night. . . . " As you describe a situation, sometimes God begins to give you his answer. Just as you are open before him with your sin, be open before him with your needs. Don't come to him with items "on demand."

One especially effective way of *describing* in prayer is to live in the presence of the situation. For instance, if someone is sick, imagine and pray through a sequence of events that will make your praying real. If you are praying for someone in the hospital, see the Lord coming to his bedside and standing by him, looking down at him, and loving him. What you're doing, in effect, is describing your prayer. You see Jesus coming to your sick friend's bedside, reaching out to take his hand, looking into his eyes, setting his hand on the aching head, and speaking words of encouragement and healing. This is not a magic formula, but it's a way of making your time with the Lord real and personal.

Most of us have at least one painful relationship in our lives right now. Apply the process of imaginative description when you pray about that relationship. Don't say, "Lord, straighten out my husband. He is such a bore and so irritable. And straighten me out because I can't control my temper." Instead, go through the circumstances in which you feel frustrated, angry, or hurt. Describe them to God. See the Lord standing there with you as you complain about your husband coming home late one more time, or when you feel angry because he doesn't seem to understand your stresses and the hard work you do each day at home, because he's preoccupied with his work at the plant or at the office. Go through that circumstance in your mind with the Lord.

There are so many people you can pray for in this way: the man in your office whom you can't stand, the woman at your church who's gossiping about you, the neighbor you want to become a believer. Pray imaginatively and descriptively, seeing the Lord coming to them, working in those arguments, and working in their circumstances. Describe it all to God.

Everything

The last letter is *E*. *E* is for *everything*. Bring everything to God. Nothing is too small for God. The Scriptures instruct us, "In every thing, give thanks" (1 Thess. 5:18 KJV).

Your daily life is not usually made up of cataclysmic events! But the momentous events and opportunities are conditioned by how you live out the small, seemingly trivial tasks and aspects of your day-to-day living. It's quite amazing when you think about a casual word or decision that ends up becoming something extraordinary. For instance, someone asked me to go to Colorado to observe Young Life's youth ministry. I had recently arrived from England and didn't want to miss an opportunity to see the Colorado Rockies, so off I went to Colorado. The first person my eyes fell on at the meal table when we sat down that first evening is the girl who is now my wife. The invitation was to go and see some youth work, but I ended up with a wife and four kids! Out of a casual invitation and response came more joy than I ever could have anticipated.

God is not too big and too busy for the little things of your life. He says the very hairs of your head are numbered, and not even a sparrow falls to the ground that he doesn't know about (see Matt. 10:29–30). If he knows and cares about your wispy hairs and little sparrows, don't you suppose he cares for all the elements of your life? You know how to do good things for your children; certainly your heavenly Father knows best how to help you (see Matt. 7:11). So bring everything. He knows, as you know, in any relationship "little things mean a lot."

Under *everything*, I want to remind you that Scripture instructs us to "give thanks in everything." We have already associated thanksgiving with adoration, but it belongs in the "everything" category as well. Having shared everything with God, it is easy to neglect to thank him—to be forever asking, but never saying "thank you." It's just like the ten lepers who were healed by the Lord Jesus (see Luke 17:11–19). You know they were all exhilarated and ran home to show off their healed wounds and share the joy of restored health. They were grateful. But only one went back to Jesus to say, "Thank you"—and Jesus noticed it! He asked, "Were not ten cleansed? Where are the nine?" (Luke 17:17).

As parents, aren't you impressed whenever your kids thank you for something they usually take for granted: "Thank you, Mom, that was a terrific meal"? Or, "Thanks, Dad, for shopping with me today"? So often they seem to thank us only for the exceptional things. We've become a rather thankless society. I saw a poster that said, "Unhappy is the man who has no one to whom to say thank you." I would change that poster to read, "Miserable is the man who never says thank you." Thank the Lord for everything— the bad as well as the good, the painful as well as the pleasant. In everything, give thanks.

For instance, cars are a constant source of irritation. My car always gives us trouble. Invariably, I get in the car to go to town and find the gas gauge on empty. What do you do with these real-life aggravations? If you don't process them properly, your day becomes a stream of misery because irritants are ever present. I have to train myself to give thanks in everything. And it isn't always easy. But when I do—it works!

Some Practical Tips

Having gone through the principles and conditions of prayer, let me give you some practical tips.

First, get yourself a little notebook and divide it into sections labeled Monday, Tuesday, Wednesday, Thursday, etc. There are so many needs and requests, you can't pray for every person and every pressing request every day. You would literally never get off your knees! Be practical and space it throughout the week. In my notebook under different days, I have the family—not just my immediate family, but my brothers and sisters and relatives. I've listed people with whom I work. I've listed former staff members, too, people who worked with me in Pittsburgh but have gone on to other places. I also pray by using my calendar. For example, on Mondays, I pray through the events of the week and look ahead to scheduled events.

A friend of mine lists not only the requests, but the *answers* to prayer. List answers to prayer in your book so you're not forever asking without thanking the Lord. You will see how God answers prayer and you will be amazed! Remember the old song, "Count your blessings, name them one by one, and it will surprise you what the Lord has done." That's sound advice! When you start saying thank you one by one, it will astound you what God has done.

Another friend prays by pictures, keeping them all over the walls of his office. That's a wonderful aid to imaginative and descriptive prayer because you can see the people you are praying for and easily imagine them. I know of one family with small children that has placed pictures on a bulletin board. The children point to choose out of their whole galaxy of friends and family whom they will pray for. There are many creative helps for your prayer life.

And finally, get yourself a place that is your prayer place. I loved going to St. Stephen's, my former church, when it was empty. It seemed the church was full of people, although it was empty and quiet, because it was full of people in my mind's eye—people who came to know the Lord there, who grew in the Lord there, who found husbands or wives there, and who brought their children there, and some who were buried and have been gone for years from there. St. Stephen's was a special place for me, a place where God ministered to me. He met me and so many others there. Get yourself a place which is your "prayer closet." And then go into your corner and pray.

May God make us all prayer warriors—people who know how to pray and never lose sight of that first principle: Prayer is primarily a relationship. Remember this chorus from the hymn, "He walks with me and He talks with me, and he tells me I am his own, and the voice I hear falling on my ear none other has ever known." God walks with us and talks with us, *personally*, in our needs and our circumstances. Prayer is the living out of a personal relationship with a loving, heavenly Father.

5

Three: Exercise Worship

And day and night they never cease to sing,
"Holy, holy, holy, is the Lord God Almighty, who
was and is and is to come!"

(Rev. 4:8b)

That's the Way God Made Us

God made each one of us for a special purpose. Every
member of the human race was created to worship. And if
we will not worship God, we will worship someone else or
something else. No matter where you look in the world, we
all worship.

I once took my daughter Chelsea and a friend to meet
the Pittsburgh Steelers when I was a chapel speaker for one
of their games. You cannot imagine the anticipation and ex-
pectancy of that day—not only mine but also the girls'. They
were so excited at the prospect of being in the same room
with their football heroes. We all have a natural tendency
to hero-worship.

I've also attended the National Prayer Breakfast in
Washington, D. C., which the president of the United
States attends. There are several thousand people, and the
excitement level is incredible when the president makes
his appearance. Why do people go? Many are there just to
see, and be in the same room with, the president.

Across the board—whether it's music, sports, politics, or something else—whenever there is a great personage present, it evokes a sense of respect, a sense of awe and admiration.

I've seen very large groups overtaken by this sense of celebrity enthusiasm. One of the most notable occasions was when Daryl Stingley, a football player who was paralyzed from the neck down, made his first public appearance after that football accident at a Monday Night Football game that was broadcast on television. Daryl Stingley was in the stadium for a game between the New England Patriots and the Buffalo Bills. Before the game began, when all the players were on the field, the referees in position, and the cameras all lined up, they announced that Daryl Stingley was in the press box. That whole stadium—thousands of people—immediately rose to its feet and began to cheer and applaud. The officials wanted to get on with the game, but they couldn't. They appealed to the crowd to stop cheering, but the crowd would not stop. And even in my own home, miles away where I was watching the little square picture of my television screen, I was caught up with the excitement and adulation of that moment.

"Football fans on a Sunday afternoon often reflect a truer attitude of worship than the average Christian. The football worshiper attends faithfully every Sunday. Oblivious to those around him, he concentrates intently on the object of his worship. He has prepared all week for this moment. He has read about the one he adores. He has talked about this day with others. And when he leaves hours later, his face is aglow with praise and thanksgiving for what he has experienced. His team won, 13 to 10" (Excerpted from "Closer Walk," *Walk Through the Bible Ministries*).

When the worship of God is superseded by the worship of a game, something is desperately wrong. But worship comes naturally to us; we *will* worship something. We may worship football, our careers, our husbands or wives, our children, or our bodies. Even self-love is very apparent in our society today.

We *will* worship because God has made us to worship. The growing Christian must become involved in the whole-hearted worship of the Lord. The central focus of a person's life was meant to be the worship of Almighty God. And when we do not worship him, or *will not* worship him, we find substitutes.

1 Chronicles 16:28–30 says,

> Ascribe to the LORD, O families of the peoples,
>   ascribe to the LORD glory and strength!
> Ascribe to the LORD the glory due his name;
>   bring an offering and come before him!
> Worship the LORD in holy array;
>   tremble before him, all the earth;
> yea, the world stands firm,
>   never to be moved.

And the next verses go on with this call to worship God. Worship is described with this term: *ascribe to the Lord*. What does *ascribe* mean? To tell forth his worthiness.

The derivation of the word *worship* is "worth-ship." Worshiping is telling forth the worthiness of God, ascribing to the Lord the glory due his name.

Revelation 4:6–11 provides a description of the worship of heaven:

> And round the throne, on each side of the throne are four living creatures, full of eyes in front and behind: the first living creature like a lion, the second living creature like an ox, the third living creature with the face of a man, and the fourth living creature like a flying eagle. And the four living creatures, each of them with six wings, are full of eyes all around and within, and day and night they never cease to sing,

> "Holy, holy, holy, is the Lord God Almighty,
> who was and is and is to come!"

And whenever the living creatures give glory and honor and thanks to him who is seated on the throne, who lives for ever and ever, the twenty-four elders fall down before him who is seated on the throne and worship him, who lives for ever and ever; they cast their crowns before the throne, singing,

> "Worthy art thou, our Lord and God,
> to receive glory and honor and power,
> for thou didst create all things,
> and by thy will they existed and were created."

The whole of creation is symbolized in those living creatures. The lion represents wild animals, and the ox represents tame animals. The creature with the face of a man represents humanity, and the eagle all flying animals. The twenty-four elders, symbolic of Old and New Testament authority, bow down to worship and tell God that he is worthy to receive glory and honor. They tell forth God's worth.

So the primary factor of worship is that we ascribe to God his greatness. This is not so much thanking him for what he has done, although everything that he has done is a reflection of his greatness. We are primarily telling him how great he is. We address him, his personage, and ascribe the glory and honor that is due his name.

All Eyes on Him

One of the marks of true worship is that you climb out of yourself and get into God. We need to become more engrossed with him than we are with what he has done for us or what we are asking him to do for us. We need to be engrossed with God himself. As long as the worshiper is wrapped up with himself and his own concerns, he is a baby.

We begin to grow up spiritually when our worship passes from thanksgiving or petition to admiration.

We are all suspicious of anybody who uses us. When we are used, we feel abused. We like to be admired for who we are, not just what we do.

Of course there is a direct relationship between who we are and what we do. God has created that relationship and made us workers. But when the expression of that admiration moves from the thing we've done to who we are as the doer, we really feel admired and loved. We want our children, for instance, to love us for who we are, not just for what we have done for them.

The dictionary definition of admiration says: "to regard with wondering esteem accompanied by pleasure and delight." Have you ever been regarded with wondering esteem, with pleasure and delight? If you haven't I'm sure you'd like to be. From a human point of view, it makes all the difference when you are loved and admired for who you are.

But when you transpose that concept, that relationship, to God Almighty, you discover that God doesn't want a recitation of all that he has done—he knows it very well. Worshiping God is distinct from ascribing worth to human beings because God doesn't need our affirmation in order to feel he is something special. The Scripture says, "Day and night they never cease to sing" (Rev. 4:8). The adoration of God never stops in heaven. So he doesn't need another million or two to applaud and say, "You're great, God" to be affirmed and become something he wasn't.

The truth is the reverse. When we worship God and give him the glory due his name, we become something special. Because God is the author and creator of humanity, he made us with a built-in need to worship. When we do not give it to God himself, we are the losers, not God. When we give our worship to something less than God, like another human being or a material item, we become something less than God intended us to be.

Changed into His Likeness

There is a sense in which we become what we worship. Jeremiah 2:4 says, "[They] went after worthlessness and became worthless." The passage goes on to say, "[They] went after things that do not profit" (Jer. 2:8). These people gave their lives, their service, their worship to things that did not count. And verse 11 tells the rest: "But my people have changed their glory for that which does not profit."

The recurring theme is that if you go after worthlessness, you will become worthless. If you give yourself to things that do not profit, you become unprofitable. If you worship less than God himself you will become less than God intended you to be.

God desires that we worship him. Not simply because it's nice for God, but because it is imperative for us. God created us to worship him.

There are two parts to worship. One is the admiration of our hearts, and the second is the praise of our lips and the praise of our lives. It is not enough just to worship God in our hearts. Our worship must be expressed on our lips and in our lives.

The Scripture says *ascribe* to God—proclaim, announce, tell forth—the glory that is due him. We need to be *expressive* about the worship of God. When we discussed prayer I encouraged you to verbalize your prayers. Worship should also go beyond the internal. There should be an extroverted, explicit expression of heartfelt worship of the Lord on our lips and in our lives.

Something marvelous happens when we worship God. We begin to reflect what God is like. We start becoming more like him. This principle is sometimes true in human nature, as well. Have you ever noticed how couples who really love each other begin to look more and more like each other? They become like the thing that they worship, love, and adore. There is a sense in which a husband and wife become more and more alike, more and more *one*, as God intended them to become.

2 Corinthians 3:18 says, "And we all, with unveiled face, beholding the glory of the Lord, are being changed into his likeness from one degree of glory to another; for this comes from the Lord who is the Spirit." When we behold Jesus, we are changed from one degree of glory to another. That word *beholding* doesn't simply mean "looking at"; the meaning is closer to "reflecting," as in a mirror. When you look at the Lord, when you behold God, you begin to *reflect* his likeness.

Our lives are like mirrors. We reflect what we worship. You reflect the people you hang around with. Your face begins to express whatever it is you give your attention to, what you live for. So as we behold the glory or the dignity of God and dwell on it, we begin to reflect Christ's likeness. You are changed from one degree of glory to another, so spend time in adoration and worship.

Imitation Is the Real Thing

When we spend time dwelling on someone, we not only reflect unconsciously what they are like but we also begin to imitate deliberately what they are like. When you adore or worship, you say, "You are great. You are wonderful." But you also find yourself saying, "I want to be like you!" Part of worship is imitation.

Young people long to be like the friends they admire and hang around with. When you "hang around with Jesus," you will want to be like him. You will choose to do the things he does. That's why reading Scripture is so important—it teaches us more about the character and qualities of our God. That is why dwelling on the Lord in prayer is so all-important. In all these ways—Scripture reading, prayer, and study, whether a personal time of study or listening to someone teach—God has given us the means to dwell on the person of Jesus Christ so we can imitate him.

Most skills are more caught than taught. You become a better piano player partly by listening to good pianists, not only by hearing what a teacher tells you. An aspiring violinist watches and listens to great violinists. A good teacher not only teaches verbally but demonstrates as well.

As a lad, I was crazy, absolutely crazy, about soccer. Since coming to the United States, I have lost my worship for soccer and soccer players because I have not been in a country where soccer is all-important, where you feed on it every weekend, and where you are saturated with the glory of it in the media. I was pretty good at the game I loved and played on a team that made it to an All-England championship. We lost, but being number two wasn't so bad! When I was a boy, I imitated great soccer players, their personalities as well as the way they played soccer.

Since my goal was to be a great soccer hero, I emulated Eric Farr, imitating his walk, so that I might become a great soccer player!

Look back over your own life. I'm sure you have imitated people you admire. As Christians, our goal is to follow Christ, to be like him. So we have to "admire" him—ascribe glory to him, *worship* him. By worshiping him, we pursue genuine imitation of Jesus Christ.

Life-style Worship

When we talk about worship, we are not just talking about going to church. Worship isn't only something you do one hour each Sunday morning. Worship is a life-style. It's something we should do all the time. We need to be constantly looking at everything we do so that we might worship in everything we do and are. 1 Corinthians 10:31 explains it simply: "Whatever you do, do all to the glory of God." Don't just sing hymns and psalms or pray prayers in church to the glory of God. *Whatever you do,* do it to God's glory so that your life becomes a worshipful expression in every detail. The most ordinary tasks and events become dignified when offered to God as an act of worship.

All of life can be glorifying to the Lord. I learned this lesson from my friend Florence who worked in England with Joan Thomas, the wife of Major Ian Thomas. Major Ian Thomas, a man who has had a great impact throughout the world, began an organization called "Torch Bearers" to evangelize the youth of Europe. Its headquarters was in a castle-like old mansion with a cobblestone courtyard and an imposing Gothic arch gateway. I used to take young people there for a week to learn about the Lord Jesus. What a marvelous place!

But even more marvelous than the beauty of the location was the attitude of the workers there. The major's wife and my friend Florence used to clean the rooms to prepare for the next group of young people coming in. And Mrs. Thomas would say to Florence, "Let's clean this room as if the Lord himself were going to sleep here tonight." Now that attitude transforms changing bed linens and dusting corners into worship. We show God's "worthship" by what we do for him. Do we have that attitude about our work?

The most ordinary task or event can glorify Jesus when done for him. Scripture tells us not to work as men-pleasers, but to work to please the Lord (see Gal. 1:10). It doesn't matter whether it's cleaning rooms, writing letters, or driving a car. The ordinary things we take for granted can become acts of worship. The goal is to have our whole lives express the glory of God!

What about Sunday Morning?

I do want to focus on the formal act of corporate worship that takes place on Sunday morning. God does call us to gather for worship. Worship was not meant to be done completely on your own.

There are some who say they can worship God better on a golf course than in a church. Others say their hearts are nearer to God in a garden than in a church. What does that say about our modern-day churches? Everything. It should never be true that people cannot worship in the church, or we are in a sad state of disobedience to God. He calls us to assemble there together, as his people. Hebrews 10:24–25 says,

> And let us consider how to stir up one another to love and good works, not neglecting to meet together, as is the habit of some, but encouraging one another, and all the more as you see the Day drawing near.

Psalm 122:1 says this: "I was glad when they said to me, 'Let us go to the house of the LORD!'" It doesn't say, "I was glad when I said, 'I'm going up to church to be by myself with God, uninterrupted by all those other noisy people around me who keep interfering with my worship.'" Those criticisms are commonly expressed. But that isn't what this portion of Psalm 122 is saying. "I was glad when they said to me, 'Let us go to the house of the Lord.'" This represents a call to corporate worship, the celebration of God's people coming together.

There is quite a difference in watching football in a stadium that will hold fifty thousand but with only five hundred people present, and watching a football game with sixty thousand crammed into that same stadium. When you are crowded in with lots of people, your attitude toward whatever it is you've gone to see, listen to, or admire is transformed. God has made us to worship him in private *and* in a corporate gathering of celebration.

I have categorized three important ingredients for Sunday morning formal worship. Let's take a look at them.

Anticipation

First, the Psalmist says, "I was glad when they said to me, 'Let us go.'" Already his juices were flowing with anticipation. As he thought about it, gladness filled his heart. It wasn't when he walked through the temple doors that he said, "Ah, now that I'm here, I can worship." On his way there, he was glad!

The following verse says, "Our feet have been standing within your gates, O Jerusalem!" (Ps. 122:2). The closer the psalmist got, the more he loved it. There are psalms called the psalms of ascent; the anticipation builds as the worshipers go up the hill to Jerusalem. Psalm 122 is an example: "Jerusalem, built as a city which is bound firmly together, to which the tribes go up" (v. 3). The people are filled with joy at being close to the temple, and they celebrate because they can assemble there to worship.

We need to encourage that sense of anticipation for ourselves. Too often, discouraging things happen before we ever get to church. Maybe you had to press and dress your husband to get him into the car. Then you pushed the kids through the bathroom and breakfast and stuffed them in the car. You had to drive over the speed limit to get to church on time. And you thought, "If only I'd gotten up earlier!" So what happens? In your frustration, you grouch at the children, "We wouldn't be late if you kids had put out your clothes like I told you to last night!" It's a shame to arrive at church emotionally warped.

But somehow, that short walk from your car through the parking lot to the church doors helps turn you around. You step out of the car, see all those other people, and suddenly you become gracious and smiling. Your poor kids wonder, "What transformed Dad?" and, "Oh, sure. *Now* Mom's in a good mood."

Seeing your fellow worshipers helps, but there are other encouragements. I recommend worshiping with music at home before church. Play the great music of the church, like Handel's "Messiah." Or play some other music that helps you anticipate worship. Pray about what will take place in the service that day. As you brush your teeth, fix your hair, and get yourself organized, be in an attitude of prayer asking the Lord to make this service like no other service. Anticipate!

One of the most solemn and sacred moments of worship in the church where I serve is when we first kneel down. One of the lovely acts of worship, which is a preparation for corporate worship, is that moment of quiet between you and the Lord in the pew before the service begins. You gather all the fractured, fragmentary thoughts into the presence of God to prepare your heart. I encourage you to be in church early for that purpose. If you have five minutes, use it on your knees before God and not in talking to someone else in the back of the church. Your purpose for being there is the worship of God Almighty. So take time to prepare yourself, and you will sense the anticipation growing in those moments.

In those five minutes, pray: "Lord, be glorified in the singing of hymns this morning. God, meet us and hear us as we pray together today. Father, bless the pastor with wisdom and truth as he preaches. God, stimulate anticipation in us!"

Concentration

Second, we will not worship if we don't concentrate. But concentrating takes work. Too many come to church wondering what it will do for *them*. The services become almost a form of entertainment. Was the choir good this morning? How about the selection of hymns? Was the preaching any good?

I didn't go to church while I was growing up, so personally I'm not familiar with this experience. But a friend told me that in his childhood, on Sundays they went to church, and then they "had the preacher sliced for lunch and cold for supper!" That family's focus was on what the church was going to do for them, not on worship of God—on what they *got*, not on what they *gave*.

When you come with that attitude, you are testing your emotional thermometer to determine whether the service is good worship or not. What we should do instead is give our *minds* to worship. We're instructed to love God with all our hearts, all our minds, and all our strength. That's pretty all-encompassing.

In Latin, the word *liturgy* actually means "work." Worship is *work*, not entertainment. We have to come to worship with a commitment to work at worship.

In the Episcopal church, we sit for instruction, kneel for prayer, and stand for praise. We structure the service that way on purpose because the physical action reminds us of what we should be doing, what we should focus on, at that particular moment in the service.

Don't let the first hymns of the service be a warm-up for real worship. Be ready to begin that first hymn with a burst of praise. When that hymn is announced, be ready to sing with all your heart! Don't be distracted by the fact that the little choirboy who just went by was wearing sneakers instead of dress shoes. It takes concentration and work to bring our minds to worship. If we always began the service with our whole minds and spirits ready to worship, our worship services would be transformed instead of starting tepidly and insipidly, as they often do. Say, "Lord, open our lips, and our mouth shall show forth your praise!"

Ecclesiastes 9:10 is one of the verses that is a key to my whole life: "Whatever your hand finds to do, do it with your might." In colloquial terms, God is telling us to "Go for it!" Give yourself to worship as enthusiastically and aggressively as you do your work, your hobby, athletics—whatever you apply yourself to.

Worship is serious business. When we take the name of the Lord on our lips in worship but do not have him in our minds and give him our attention, there is a sense in which we take the name of the Lord in vain. It's a misconception that we must take to the streets and curse to take the name of the Lord in vain. Mouthing words in a worship service without giving our attention to what they say is quite enough. God commands us to honor his name, not to take it lightly, so give your attention and your concentration to the *work* of worship.

Imagination

Third, God made human beings different from the rest of creation. He gave us imaginations so that we could bring to mind things that we cannot see, so that we could *imagine* them. Without the gift of imagination, we could not worship. How can we worship a God who we cannot see, unless "by faith" we use our imaginations to "behold him."

I love to think about the angels, the archangels, and the whole company of heaven, magnifying his glorious name, saying, "Holy, holy, holy!" In my imagination, I join the company of heaven. I see the Lord enthroned, high and lifted up. I see all of heaven rejoicing and worshiping. I even picture loved ones who have gone on to heaven, worshiping there in the company of heaven, praising Jesus. I join them! Without an imagination, you cannot worship in this way.

The imagination is a marvelous tool for adoring and worshiping God. When you kneel to pray, picture yourself kneeling before God as if he were seated in glory and crowned before you. Imagination can transform your worship.

The rest of chapter four of Revelation talks about God's voice being like rolling thunder and going forth as lightning. Don't picture God as some placid old man, benign and loving, sitting up there like Santa Claus with white hair and a beard, patting you on the head. He's more like roaring thunder and flashing lightning! Use Scripture and your imagination in your worship.

The Overarching Principle

So what is the overarching principle of worship? That it includes the whole of your life. Unless you are prepared to worship God with all of your life, you will find it nearly impossible to worship God for that one hour on Sunday morning. You will feel phony and hypocritical coming to worship for that hour when you have been blasé to God with your life all week. The same Spirit of God that brought you to new life in Christ and indwells you and makes you a new person will help you need and desire worship. So ask the Lord to fill you with his Holy Spirit as you learn to show forth his "worthship" in every aspect of your day-to-day life.

6

Four: Share Your Faith

For I am not ashamed of the gospel; it is the power of God for salvation to every one who has faith.

(Rom. 1:16)

When you come to know Jesus Christ, many things are new to you. The Bible becomes vibrantly alive. Worship is a colorful, life-molding experience. Prayer is eye-opening, something brand new to you. And now you can even share your relationship with Jesus Christ with other people. What joy!

But what do we mean by sharing your faith? We call this *witnessing* or *evangelizing*. Witnessing is introducing others to the Lord Jesus whom you have come to know. It comes naturally to every Christian believer. New Christians may not be very good at it, but witnessing is something that, in their hearts, they want to do.

If we are committed to growing in our Christian lives, applying ourselves to the business of sharing our faith is one of the best beginning places. There are several reasons why you should *witness* for the Lord.

For Yourself

Scripture gives us the first reason why we should share our faith: when you witness you seal your relationship to Jesus Christ. Romans 10:9 says, "Because, if you confess with your lips that Jesus is Lord and believe in your heart that God raised him from the dead, you will be saved." And verse 10 explains it further: "For man believes with his heart and so is justified, and he confesses with his lips and so is saved." These verses tie together what we believe in our hearts and what we say with our lips. The implication is that belief in your heart is not enough; you must also share with your lips. That verbal affirmation seals and confirms your relationship with Jesus Christ and your new life in him.

The first time I fell in love I was about fourteen years old. Her name was Brenda Watts. It was so difficult to tell her I loved her! It was one thing to have the love in my heart, but to get it out on my lips and then say it to her was just impossible. But with my wife, Kathie, it was different. When I finally managed to tell her that I loved her, the saying of the words settled and confirmed my love.

There are many people who cannot enjoy their relationship with Jesus Christ because they've never come out in the open and verbalized it. Their faith is shrouded in doubt, agnosticism, and uncertainty. They keep questioning, always worrying whether they really believe or not, or whether they believe enough or not. One solution to much of this ambiguity is to communicate their love for Jesus Christ verbally.

So this first reason for sharing our faith is a selfish one: testifying to our faith settles it for *us*. It is good for us— good for our own subjective, emotional security in our new life with Christ.

There's No Other Plan

The second and more important reason to "witness" is that we are instructed to do so by Jesus. He *commanded* us to share our faith with others. When Jesus called his disciples, what did he say to them? Some of them were fishermen. He said, "Follow me and I will make you become fishers of men" (Mark 1:17). That was the understanding on which they joined his team. His last words reiterate the earlier instruction: "Go into all the world and preach the gospel" (Mark 16:15). "Go therefore and make disciples of all nations" (Matt. 28:19). And, right before his ascension, Jesus told the disciples, "But you shall receive power when the Holy Spirit has come upon you; and you shall be my witnesses in Jerusalem and in all Judea and Samaria and to the end of the earth" (Acts 1:8). Jesus began and ended his ministry here on earth with the important command to his followers to be fishers of men and women, to go preach the gospel, to be *witnesses.* By obeying his command, we please Jesus.

There are really only two responses to a command—to obey it or to disobey it. The Christian who is eager to grow in Christ must do what Christ says. We need to obey—not just because it's good for us, but because God left Christians in charge of carrying out his plan for the world. Our obedience in passing on to our friends the truth of Christ is the means whereby others are going to come to know him.

What? We're the best system he could come up with? Wouldn't it be much easier for God to flash messages on a person's bedroom wall at night to tell him to become a believer? And wouldn't it make life simpler if non-Christians could somehow wander into a church by their own intuition, hear the gospel, and become believers? Wouldn't it be wonderful if a supernatural messenger would show up to witness to our husbands, children, and family? Those plans for spreading the Good News seem better to us, but God has his own agenda. The witness of his people is the Lord's plan.

Can you imagine what took place when Jesus returned to heaven from earth? Probably all the angels gathered around him. The whole company of heaven must have rejoiced to have him back. And then maybe one angel said, "What's going to happen down there now that you're here?"

"I've left those eleven men to share with the world what I have shared with them," he would have replied.

The angels almost panicked. "But what if they don't do it? What if they fail?"

And Jesus would have answered them, "I have no other plan."

There is no other plan. Romans 10:14–15 says,

> But how are men to call upon him in whom they have not believed? And how are they to believe in him of whom they have never heard? And how are they to hear without a preacher? And how can men preach unless they are sent? As it is written, "How beautiful are the feet of those who preach good news!"

It's only through his people sharing Christ's message that men and women and boys and girls will come to know him. We can be obedient to his plan and help advance his agenda in this world or we can be disobedient. The choice is ours.

To Demonstrate Love

The third reason we should be witnessing for the Lord is that it demonstrates our love for other people. It not only seals our love for the Lord, and it's not only obedience to his command; it's a demonstration that we love other people. Jesus had a great, heartbreaking love for the people to whom he ministered. "When he saw the crowds, he had compassion for them, because they were harassed and helpless, like sheep without a shepherd" (Matt. 9:36). It broke his heart to see those sheep wander aimlessly with no one to lead them. In Matthew 23:37 Jesus cried out:

> "O Jerusalem, Jerusalem, killing the prophets and stoning those who are sent to you! How often would I have gathered your children together as a hen gathers her brood under her wings, and you would not!"

Luke 10:2 puts his desire for all people to come to him so clearly that we can't avoid the message. "The harvest is plentiful, but the laborers are few; pray therefore the Lord of the harvest to send out laborers into his harvest."

As you look at the world around you, do you have this kind of compassion for those who do not know Jesus? If you want to love people and demonstrate that love, the ultimate way is to be a harvester for Jesus Christ.

We want to love people in many other ways, and we need to. People often say, "I am going to demonstrate my love for the Lord with my life. I'm going to do nice things for people and encourage them and be such a tremendous neighbor and friend that, hopefully, because of the witness of my life, one of these days they are going to come and say to me, 'What is it about you, Harry, that makes you such a terrific person? Where do you get all that love?' And then I can tell them!"

I will confess in all honesty that nobody has *ever* come to me and said that. And I have been a believer in Jesus for twenty years! I have attempted to be nice to people, to love them, and I have done some extraordinary things to demonstrate that love.

While I was living in London, an old man lived with his family in the house next door. His family had disowned him and left him in his room upstairs to fend for himself. They would do nothing for him. On one occasion he got so ill that he couldn't even get out of his room. Eventually, I couldn't stand it any longer. I went in there, and I bathed him and cleaned up all the feces and mess in that room. I even had to run out of the house because I couldn't stand the smell and filth any longer. But I went back in, finished the job, bought some flowers to brighten up that bleak place, and got him some food.

Nobody ever came to me and said, "John, that was terrific. Why did you do that? Tell me what motivated you." No one asked. But just because no one is asking or patting you on the back is no reason to keep from telling people why.

Feeding, clothing, and caring for others is wonderful and right, but it's not the ultimate way to demonstrate our love. The ultimate demonstration of our love is to introduce them to Jesus because without him they are going into an eternity of emptiness, lostness, hopelessness, and torment. And they're going to live out life on earth without knowing who they are, what they're here for, or where they're going.

I'm sure you know several people personally who try to fill their lives with money, success, sex, music, vacations, pleasure, status—everything except the Lord who *can* fill that empty space. Romans 10:14 asks the obvious questions: How are they going to hear? They won't unless somebody tells them. Who's going to tell them? Jesus has sent *us*. The greatest demonstration of love we can offer is to do what Christ commanded us.

It Comes Naturally

The fourth reason why we must share our faith is that it really is a natural outgrowth of Jesus Christ alive and at work in us.

In John 15:4, Jesus uses the analogy of the vine and the branches: "Abide in me, and I in you. As the branch cannot bear fruit by itself, unless it abides in the vine, neither can you, unless you abide in me." That word *abide* really means "engrafted." If we are engrafted into Christ, then his life flows out through us. If we are not engrafted into him, we will dry up and wither like old twigs and branches. We'll be good for nothing except firewood. "He who abides in me, and I in him, he it is that bears much fruit, for apart from me you can do nothing" (John 15:5). If we are engrafted into Jesus, we will be productive, fruitful.

That same passage in John goes on to say, "You did not choose me, but I chose you and appointed you that you should go and bear fruit and that your fruit should abide" (John 15:16). In other words, the reason that the Lord called us to himself and drew us into his life is that we might be fruitful. Granted, there are all kinds of fruits. But one of the great kinds of fruit—the fruit that comes from having Jesus in us—is reproduction in kind. We have been born to reproduce naturally; we have been born again to reproduce *super*naturally. God chose us not only for our own good but also so we would reproduce, enlarging the family of God.

Remember Jesus' words to his disciples on the day of the ascension? "You shall be my witnesses." *You shall be.* It's definitely going to happen; it will be a natural outcome of the spirit of God living in you.

The day I asked the Lord into my life, I went dancing through the streets of London. I couldn't wait to tell people my good news. And I confidently assumed that if I, John Guest—rather cool, quite an operator, an athlete, and a lot of other things—would go and tell them, they would certainly become believers, too. I wanted to share with all my friends and family. I couldn't wait to tell them, and they couldn't wait to get rid of me! I was amazed and disappointed. And then I remembered how I responded to the man who first talked to me about Jesus. I couldn't wait to get rid of him, either!

The System Works

But God's system works. Maybe the story of how I heard about God's provision for reconciliation will be an encouragement to you in this business of sharing your faith.

I was not raised religiously. Like all babies in England, I was baptized as an infant. My parents never took me to church. There were no Bibles in my home. We never prayed at meals, not even at Christmastime. I went occasionally to Sunday school when I had some new clothes, because that was the only place I was allowed to wear them. In England, there is no division of church and state, so there is some religious education in the school system. I learned a little about prayer there, and I learned the Ten Commandments, but somehow the message didn't get through too well.

As a teenager I worked with Ray Wilson, a man in his twenties, who told me one day, "John, I would just as soon you don't swear when you work with me." That was quite unusual considering that most of the men I worked with demonstrated their masculinity by cursing and swearing.

So I asked, "Why not?"

He said, "Because I'm a Christian."

"Oh well, so am I," I responded confidently.

"What makes you think you're a Christian?" he asked.

"Because I believe in God (which I did in a vague, general way) and because I'm English. England is a Christian country. All Englishmen are Christians."

"Well, that doesn't make you a Christian." And he proceeded to make it plain why it didn't.

I was getting curious. "So what makes you one and me not one?"

He was ready for that question. "Well, take the word *Christian*. It really says Christ-ian. A Christian is someone whose life really revolves around Jesus Christ—you know, in the same way a soccer player's revolves around soccer."

He definitely had my number now because I lived, breathed, slept, and ate with the purpose of becoming a great soccer player. I immediately understood the commitment involved in being a Christian, and I knew I wasn't one.

When I left Oxford where I'd met Ray Wilson, I went through my training to be an engineer in London, and finally ended up in seminary in Bristol. One day I remembered Ray's witness and wanted to let him know how my life had changed. I wanted to thank him. I had laughed at him, rejected what he said, and asked him all kinds of tricky, nasty questions. But all the while I was learning what it meant to be a Christian—that Jesus loved *me*, John Guest, enough to die for me on the cross to take away the penalty that's mine as a sinner. I had fallen short of the glory of God, but Jesus made it possible for me to be forgiven and to know for sure that my home was in heaven and that my life could be abundant and fulfilled. Whew! It was amazing—Ray Wilson got all that through to me! So I sent him a note to thank him.

After I was ordained, I took one summer to preach at a church at the seaside, and invited an old childhood friend of mine from Oxford to spend some time with me at the shore. I hadn't seen him since I was about fifteen. He came with his wife and their son, David, to stay near where I was to minister. He came and heard me preach and afterward he asked, "How did this happen?" I told him that I found that life became more and more empty the more I tried to fill it with pleasure.

"You know, I found that same thing," he said. "I'm married and I love my wife. I've got my little boy, a new house, a car, and a good job. But there's something missing."

I began to share with him what that missing piece was. One evening I took that family to hear an English preacher. Because their son, David, was too young and unused to that sort of thing, I took him out of the meeting. We walked around Bristol and saw the ships that came into the center of the city. We got back about the time I thought the meeting would end and found the place filled to capacity. Our places had been taken so we stood at the top of the aisle as the people sang, "Just as I am without one plea, but that thy blood was shed for me, and that thou bidst me come to thee, Oh Lamb of God, I come." Then the preacher invited the people to come forward to demonstrate their commitment to Christ. During the next verse, my friends went forward. Little David thought they were leaving. He shot out of my hand and down the aisle about the time they got to the front, and grabbed his mother's skirt. She turned around and picked him up. There they were, a brand new family in Christ.

A year later I visited their home. He was helping with the young people at their church; she was teaching Sunday school. And little David was singing, "Jesus loves me, this I know" instead of, "She loves you, yea! yea! yea!"

A couple of years later I took those friends to Oxford and knocked at Ray Wilson's door. I told them, "This is the man who first talked to me about Jesus." We were a line of three, and I've often wondered since then how long the line at Ray Wilson's door is by now. Those friends of mine are now in Australia, where he does some lay preaching, adding to the line standing at Ray Wilson's door.

How long is the line at your door? What have you reproduced through Christ living in you? Like begets like. When the church isn't reproducing it shrivels up in atrophy. But when we are obeying God's command, we're growing and blossoming.

Three Kinds of Evangelism

I have separated the ways to share your faith into three broad categories. I hope these classifications will help you think about how you can be involved in testifying to the truth about Christ.

Personal invitation

First of all, the simplest kind of evangelism is what I call *personal invitation.* Personally invite people to come with you to church, where they can hear the preaching of the Good News. Invite them to hear speakers who have a gift for communicating that Good News. Invite them to read a book that testifies about the gospel. You could leave a modern translation of the New Testament with them and encourage them to read it.

I gave my own brother Tony the *J. B. Phillips* translation of the New Testament. He didn't pick it up until about a year later. He was about thirty-eight at the time. But he finally started and read four or five chapters of Matthew.

Suddenly, he heard a voice say to him audibly, "You know Jesus is my son." He looked around to see if his children had heard it, but they hadn't. His wife in the kitchen hadn't, either. He went upstairs and knelt by his bed, and his life flew before him in his mind. He said, "I wept for the lost years." Now that dramatic a conversion is rare, but keep on giving friends the Bible. The Lord speaks from his Word.

I think the greatest vehicle for personal invitation is the home. Invite people into your home. Let them observe the quality of life in your home, the difference the Lord has made in your home, the sense of love, caring, and sharing that only being a part of the family of God brings. Before I was even a Christian, I was determined that the home I would establish as a parent would be different than the one in which I grew up. I didn't know *how* it was going to be different, but I knew I wanted it to be different. Because of Christ, our home offers a tremendous opportunity to invite people in—Christians and non-Christians.

Before my brother Tony had that experience of meeting the Lord while reading the Gospel of Matthew, he visited me here in the United States. I did a rather awful thing to him during that visit. I invited Christian friends over all at once and introduced them to Tony by having them tell how they had come to know the Lord. He sat and listened to them share one after the other how Christ had brought them to himself. After spending a month with me, playing on the beaches of Florida and golfing on some of the most beautiful courses, he said that the evening with my friends was the most meaningful experience of the trip. Now that is God working through inviting people in!

Personal witness

The second type of evangelism is *personal witness*. Explain what God has done for you. Tell about your personal experience with him. Christian witnessing is like giving testimony in court. Witnessing is bearing witness, giving a testimony of your experience of the love of Jesus Christ in your life. Almost anybody can do that! You bear witness simply by sharing what God has done in *your* life.

Hard-core evangelism

The third type of evangelism is sharing what God has done for *them*. I call it *hard-core evangelism*. Hard-core evangelism goes beyond telling what God has done for you. This is telling others what God has done for them, that God loves them, that Jesus Christ died for them, that he took their sins away, that he's there in the power of his spirit wanting to come into their lives, that they can invite him in. You ask them if they would like to give their lives over to Christ. You invite them to pray with you toward that end.

Objections Overruled

I want to encourage you by answering some objections you might have to doing these kinds of evangelism. There are three main reasons why people say they can't or shouldn't witness, and most of you will identify with them.

I don't know enough

The first one is: *I don't know enough.* My answer to that objection is that you will *never* know enough to answer all the questions people have because they will ask you more questions than you can answer.

I've been to theological school and have been a minister for over twenty years, and people *still* ask me questions for which I have no answer. Some questions just don't have answers. For example, no one knows where outer space ends—it doesn't. There is no answer to the question, "Where does space lead to?" If people can't comprehend space, they won't understand eternity. And if we can't understand space or eternity, how are we supposed to have all the answers about the God who is bigger than all of it?

The only one who has all the answers is God. If we had all the answers, we'd be God. So relax and know that you will never have all the answers.

On the other hand, it is possible to get *some* answers. Learn how to share your faith. Don't hide behind the excuse, "I don't know enough." You can learn a lot! 1 Peter 3:15 says, "Always be prepared to make a defense to any one who calls you to account for the hope that is in you, yet do it with gentleness and reverence."

It's not difficult to share with someone the information that he needs to know. You may not know all the answers to their questions, but if you have come to Christ you already know enough for them to do the same. The information that got you there is information they probably don't have.

I don't want to offend anyone

But there's another excuse: *I don't want to offend anyone.* Like the first excuse, this is a genuine reason. Not only do you not have all the information you need to answer all their questions, you are afraid of turning people off so that they will never want to hear the Good News again.

The chances are that if they're turned off, it won't be because of you. It will be because of the message. Think of your own experience. Were you offended the first time someone told you about Christ and your need for salvation? I was. But I *needed* to be told—my life hinged on it. So fear of offending someone isn't a good enough reason.

People were offended at Jesus all the time. Even though his communication was always perfect, he always loved them perfectly, and his motives were always perfect, they still turned him off and rejected him. He irritated them to no end. So some offenses can't be avoided. There will be people who are irritated and put off, but for most people that is a necessary step of coming to a place of giving their lives to Christ.

I am ashamed

The third reason cuts to the heart of the matter: *we are ashamed.* We are afraid of what people will think of us. When we get right down to it, we are the centers of our own worlds. We are more worried about what others think about us than with their knowing Christ and receiving the gift of eternal life. We are more determined to protect our lives and remain invulnerable than we are to have them come into the rich fulfillment of Jesus and all the joy, peace, and love that he can bring. We love ourselves more than we love them. We love ourselves more than the Lord who has commanded us to share the gospel with them.

In Romans 1:16, Paul says, "For I am not ashamed of the gospel: it is the power of God for salvation to every one who has faith." *I am not ashamed of the gospel.* Why not? Because the gospel is the power of God to save everyone who has faith.

Jesus said these rather severe words: "Whoever is ashamed of me and of my words, of him will the Son of man be ashamed when he comes in his glory and the glory of the Father" (Luke 9:26). It's an awful thing to be ashamed of the Lord Jesus Christ. I know that shame. I have failed to share the gospel because I have been ashamed.

Dr. James Kennedy, now a pastor of a very large and well-known church (Coral Ridge Presbyterian Church in Fort Lauderdale), said that he used to have a back problem that kept him from sharing the gospel: a great yellow stripe down the middle of his back! It's not that we don't know enough, because we *do* know enough. It's our human pride. When we offend people they turn us off and we feel ashamed, isolated, and rejected. So we keep our mouths closed.

Alexander the Great, who conquered so many nations and wept when there were no more nations to conquer, could not stand cowardice. He summarily executed anyone who turned tail and ran from the battle. But one cowardly young man who had run away from the battle was also named Alexander. He was such a good-looking young man, his commanding officer was sure that Alexander the Great would let him off when he saw him and learned his name.

When he was brought to Alexander the Great, young Alexander pleaded his case and shared his fears. Alexander the Great asked him, "Young man, what is your name?"

Young Alexander thought, *Oh boy, my ace card! He'll give in when he discovers I'm named after him.* "My name is Alexander."

Alexander the Great stood up in anger and said, "Young man, change your name or change your actions!"

We call ourselves "Christians," or followers of Christ. But are we ashamed of the one we're named after? If you want to grow, change your actions—you do not have the option of changing your name.

Helpful Hints for Sharing Your Faith

Here are some helpful ideas to aid you in sharing your faith.

- Pray that the Holy Spirit would lead you to new opportunities in your travel and business. Often it's the informal circumstance that the Lord uses to follow up someone else's witness. You become one more influence that brings someone to Christ.

- Master the use of a simple gospel presentation such as the "Four Spiritual Laws" or "Steps to Peace with God" and always have them available. Carry them in your wallet, car, or purse. Be prepared!

- Write out your own account of how you became a Christian and be able to tell it in about three minutes.

- If you are in a Christian family, pray together about how you might use your home. Invite people to a meal or a Bible study or a fellowship time. During any of these someone who is known to be a Christian should be asked to tell how they became a Christian—thus creating an informal witness.

- Pray (and suggest) that your own church or Sunday school class create opportunities for evangelism and then be available to help.

- Have on hand (at home or at work) easy-to-read books or booklets that help someone think through their own relationship with the Lord.

- Read a good book on sharing your faith. (*Out of the Saltshaker and Into the World* by Becky Pippert and *Disciples Are Made—Not Born* by Walt Henrichsen are excellent.)

- Make plans to attend a seminar on witnessing with a friend. Going with a friend will encourage you to stick with your commitment.

- Pray by name for people you believe don't know Jesus, that the Holy Spirit will work in their hearts to make them receptive to your message. You may find the following helpful in organizing your prayer list.

My Prayer List

List people who you believe need to know Jesus or be recommitted to him *and* how and when you think they might be approached.

Name	*Contact Ideas*
_____	_____
_____	_____
_____	_____
_____	_____
_____	_____
_____	_____
_____	_____
_____	_____
_____	_____

These tips available from "Personal Renewal Month," a program from The John Guest Evangelistic Team, 3366 Burton St. S.E., Grand Rapids, MI 49546.

7

Five: Enjoy Fellowship

Bear one another's burdens and so fulfil the law
of Christ.

(Gal. 6:2)

Many people want to be private Christians. It's true that their relationship to the Lord is personal. But these Christians feel that their relationship with God, the vertical relationship, is the only relationship that is important. So they neglect the horizontal relationships, those of people to people. Throughout the churches in our world of Christianity, you will find a lot of people who consider themselves private Christians.

And this attitude shows clearly in their approach to Christianity and the church. They don't feel a need to be involved with other people. They talk about "My Lord, my God, my church" as if they had sole ownership, as if their Christianity is just a relationship between themselves and God.

While the vertical relationship with God is primary and ultimately most important, that relationship with God is not going to develop and flourish unless we enter into relationships with one another—that's what *fellowship* is primarily about.

Being Together, Doing Together

In Greek, there are two words which describe fellowship in the New Testament. One is the word *koinonia*, with which most Christians are familiar. Some fellowship groups in churches are called koinonia fellowships or koinonia groups. The other word, *metoche*, talks about our relationships in the horizontal community, the relationships of Christians to one another. *Koinonia* is corporate activity, joint participation with people in work projects. The second springs from the first, of course. When we have this mutual spirit, the mutual calling, fellowship is more than just being together. Fellowship becomes people *doing* things together.

Being together and doing together are fused in fellowship. Acts 2:42 describes what happened after three thousand people committed themselves to Christ on the day of Pentecost. What an incredible day! Peter preached one sermon, the very first sermon of this new community, and at least three thousand were converted. "And they devoted themselves to the apostles' teaching," but also to the apostles' fellowship. They committed themselves to hang out with the original Christians. "Devoted themselves to" is a very strong phrase. It wasn't a light relationship, it was a *committed* relationship. It wasn't just a light friendship, it was a *heavy* friendship. Through conversion to Jesus Christ, they entered into a devoted relationship, "koinonia," with the apostles.

This koinonia fellowship springs from the new family into which they had entered. Remember the definition of koinonia? Association springing from a mutual spirit. The Scriptures teach that there can be no fellowship between darkness and light (John 1:5, 3:19; Acts 26:18; 1 Peter 2:9). Those of us who are born again of God's spirit become new people. From that moment on we cannot have what the Bible calls *fellowship* with people who are from the darkness, those who have not yet entered into the light. We can have friendships with those in darkness, of course. There are other kinds of relationships that remain possible, but this devoted, committed relationship is no longer appropriate between those who are of the light, who have been born again into the fellowship of Jesus Christ, and those who are of the darkness.

We enter into the fellowship circle of Christians when we enter into a new relationship with God. The relationship with God is the impetus which changes our relationships with those around us.

We are different people after meeting Jesus. John 1:12 says, "To all who received him, who believed in his name, he gave power to become children of God." These receivers/believers became something that they were not. And once they became children of God, they exhibited a different likeness and life-style and desire. They changed. They became different people. They became "children of God; who were born, not of blood nor of the will of the flesh nor of the will of man, but of God" (John 1:13). From that new beginning between us and God we become new people, and as new people it is natural for us to enter into new sets of relationships.

"If any one is in Christ, he is a new creation; the old has passed away, behold, the new has come" (2 Cor. 5:17). Part of the old that passes away when you come to Christ is old commitments, old allegiances, and old life-styles. As new people in Christ, we take on a new way of life.

Romans 8:16–17 says, "When we cry, 'Abba! Father!' it is the Spirit himself bearing witness with our spirit that we are children of God, and if children, then heirs, heirs of God and fellow heirs with Christ." Imagine that! When we are born again of the Spirit of God and his spirit comes to indwell us, we are not only born again to a new life here, but our inheritance is the same as that of Jesus Christ! We are joint heirs with Christ. Our inheritance is the same as his because our family is the same as his and because our Father is now the same as his.

Second Peter 1:3–4 talks about what we receive when we enter the family of God:

> His divine power has granted to us all things that pertain to life and godliness, through the knowledge of him who called us to his own glory and excellence, by which he has granted to us his precious and very great promises, that through these you may escape from the corruption that is in the world because of passion, and become partakers of the divine nature.

Peter teaches us that when we enter into Christ and his spirit enters us, we become *partakers* of the divine nature. In 2 Corinthians Paul rephrases the same concept, saying that our bodies become temples of the Holy Spirit (2 Cor. 6:16).

That new family membership provides the foundation of the new fellowship, the koinonia. Having been made new in Christ, we become children of God, heirs, joint heirs with Christ, and partakers of the divine nature. So we have become new people, the old things have passed away and the new have come.

Koinonia Is Natural

The natural expression of this supernatural transformation is koinonia. When I hear of people who do not want to be with other Christians, who do not want to be intimate in their fellowship, socializing, and commitment with other Christians, I immediately question whether they have that personal relationship with God. If they want to be alone in their Christianity, they say, in effect, "I don't need you. I'm self-sufficient." I begin to question whether the spirit of God has entered into them and made them God's children because the natural thing for any family is to want to be together. Only a very sick family doesn't want to associate. The natural expression of the spirit of God indwelling us is that we want to be together.

I remember that as a brand new Christian, I just loved being with other Christians. We had a midweek Bible study and prayer meeting at my church in London. It was an oasis for me after being out with my non-Christian associates at work, school, and play. I had to continue to live in some of those associations, but now I was called to live in them differently. I was no longer part of the world, but now I was reaching out to it to change it. After being with these friends and co-workers who didn't share my life in Christ, it was marvelous to get back with my Christian family.

When I was eighteen, the young people organized themselves and began to get together on Saturday nights to do something together—something different than other young men and women normally do on Saturday nights. It was much more pleasant to be together as fellow members of the family of Jesus Christ with one Father than to be out there in the secular world alone, subjected to all the pressures of that now alien environment.

So the natural expression of the supernatural beginning, our new relationship with God, is that we want to be together. And it's in that fellowship that most of our growth takes place. We've discussed how Bible study and prayer, things we do by ourselves, help us grow, but being around other Christians is very important. Most of our growth, especially as young Christians, will come from participating in that circle of koinonia fellowship.

A Life-style of Imitation

A new life-style is as much "caught" as "taught." We learn by being around people who are more mature than we are or who are suffering as we are. As we grow together we are going to learn together what it means to follow Jesus Christ and be like him. The new beginning leads to a new behavior. The new behavior is *caught* primarily through these relationships rather than *taught*, especially in the initial stages.

In Philippians 3:17, Paul says to the members of the church at Philippi which he had planted, "Brethren, join in imitating me." He was encouraging his congregation with the idea that once you enter into fellowship with Jesus Christ and with one another, *imitation* begins. You begin to walk in the steps of your mentors, your brother and sister Christians. Paul unashamedly says, "Join in imitating me and those who live as we have lived." He is eager to keep them from falling, like so many others:

> For many, of whom I have often told you and now tell you even with tears, live as enemies of the cross of Christ. Their end is destruction, their god is the belly, and they glory in their shame, with minds set on earthly things. (Phil. 3:18–19)

What Paul is saying here is, "If you hang around with those who walk in darkness, you will end up in darkness too. So hang around with me and my friends and those who live like we do, and you will end up imitating us. Join in imitating me."

Managing Peer Pressure

Without question our peers have a profound influence on us. We spend our time with their attitudes. We absorb the character of the people we admire. Spend your time with skeptical people, and you'll become a skeptic. Spend your time with optimistic people, and you will become optimistic. Spend your time with profane people, and you'll become profane. Spend your time with people who love and pursue Jesus, and you'll find yourself living after the same fashion.

One of the sadnesses in our world today is the gross profanity that is present everywhere. It has become almost a natural way of speaking for people, an acceptable part of life. We have a lot of public profanity. People don't just swear privately in their offices or in their homes, they freely swear on buses and planes, in airports and hotels, whenever or wherever. I use profanity as one example. But if you hang around with people who've got other pursuits and other language styles, their pursuits and styles will rub off on you.

As a young boy, I hung around with some other kids who were absolutely devoted to cars. They could actually tell you what kind of car was coming along the road without even looking; they could tell by the sound of it. Part of our little game was to name the car that was coming up behind us as we walked along the street together. It became a part of my own fascination because I hung out with them. Now, there's nothing wrong with cars; this is just a neutral description. The point is, I got into what the people I hung out with were into.

So the company we keep is very important to our personal development. You hang out with people who have a heart for other people, and you gain a heart for other people. You hang out with people who are constantly ministering, reaching out, praying, visiting other people, and that will become part of your life-style.

Toward the Goal of Christian Maturity

Our maturity as Christians is closely tied to our fellowship with other Christians. Maturity does not necessarily come before knowledge. You *need* knowledge. But knowledge is not Christian maturity, *behavior* is Christian maturity. I know people who've got incredible knowledge, but yet they're incredibly immature. They have all kinds of information, but they've never put it to work. They've learned methods for sharing their faith, but they never do it! They know methods for studying the Bible, but they don't really study. They've got all the information about prayer, but they don't pray. They know all about worship, but they don't worship.

While you need the foundation of information, it's koinonia fellowship that offers you the best chance of becoming mature in your Christian faith.

Vulnerability

Maturity primarily springs from *vulnerability*. It is impossible to become a strong believer and a Christian who is "real" without getting genuinely involved with other Christians—and that means being vulnerable to them. Romans 12:15–18 says,

> Rejoice with those who rejoice, weep with those who weep. Live in harmony with one another; do not be haughty, but associate with the lowly; never be conceited. Repay no one evil for evil, but take thought for what is noble in the sight of all. If possible so far as it depends upon you, live peaceably with all.

The passage goes on to teach about how Christians ought to live together. The context of this teaching is the real knowledge of one another.

Real knowledge of one another is epitomized in the words "rejoice with those who rejoice" and "weep with those who weep." How well do you know other people, and how well do you let them rejoice with you when you rejoice, because rejoicing isn't too vulnerable most of the time. But are you ready to weep with those who weep?

Obviously if you're going to rejoice with those who really rejoice, and weep with those who really weep, you've got to be *involved* with them. And the power of that vulnerability leads us on to maturity as followers of Jesus Christ.

This is what fellowship means: Instead of being alone with my Bible and my Lord, doing my own private thing, I am open with other people in koinonia fellowship. I am devoted to them, open to them. That openness to one another leads to maturity. You will not mature as a Christian unless you get deeply involved with other Christians. Remain a completely private Christian, and you will end up with all kinds of knowledge and go through all kinds of disciplines. But you will never be the fulfilled Christian God wants you to be.

When you open yourself to other Christians, they discover who you are and are able to pray for you and encourage you. When they are open, you discover who they are and are able to minister to them, counsel them, and pray with them.

This kind of vulnerability is absolutely contrary to the secular mind-set. The motto of the world is, "Never get too deeply involved with another person." One of the great personal tragedies in our world today is that people don't know how to be intimate. They don't know how to get close. It's something we learn once we are born again of God's Spirit. Because we live very private lives, we put up fronts. Jesus is the only one who knows what's going on behind that facade. So there is much pain out there that only Jesus sees because he alone knows. That's the way the world wants it. Secular society does not want to let people in.

We have the hardest time letting others into our lives. You don't necessarily have to let *everyone* in. You'd be an open freeway! But you've got to let some in, and that's fellowship—commitment to a group of people whom you've let in to help you grow.

Accountability

Vulnerability is part of koinonia; so is *accountability*. Maturity flourishes with accountability. Listen to these words:

Brethren, if a man is overtaken in any trespass, you who are spiritual should restore him in a spirit of gentleness. Look to yourself, lest you too be tempted. Bear one another's burdens and so fulfil the law of Christ. For if anyone thinks he is something, when he is nothing, he deceives himself. (Gal. 6:1–3)

There are two accountabilities spoken of here: The fellowship is to hold us accountable, and we are to make ourselves accountable.

It's not that we just move in on one another to discipline one another when one of the fellowship is "overtaken in a trespass." It's a more natural relationship. We are to bear one another's burdens. We don't just hold one another accountable to be all that we can and should be, but we make ourselves accountable, opening ourselves to bear one another's burdens. So we are to be accountable and to be held accountable.

Nobody wants to *be* accountable and nobody wants to be *held* accountable. Nor do we want to hold other people accountable. Generally speaking, this hesitancy comes from the cowardice of the secular mind-set of the world around us. Who needs to get involved in telling someone they need to straighten up? Who needs to get involved in bearing somebody else's burden? No one outside of our new life in Christ would seek out those responsibilities. But within koinonia fellowship, the fellowship of Christ, we are to be accountable and be held accountable.

Accountability will lead us on to maturity like nothing else. Take a moment to see how you're measuring up in this area. To whom are you accountable? Who knows whether you have or do not have your personal devotion time with God? With whom do you share the major failures of your life? Who is there you can call who will really bear your burden? Who is there in your life who will come and tell you when you are wrong?

I have a friend who is very, very important in my life. Some years ago, he called me up and said, "John, I'm going to be in Boston when you're up there speaking. I want to get together and have dinner." He took me out to one of those fancy piers to a great seafood restaurant. Since he was paying, I ordered big; I was incredibly poor in those days!

During dinner, my friend told me that he could not support me in the way I was behaving. In love, he said, "John, you've got to change." The problem was my preaching style. "You have become too angry in your preaching." He was right—I was.

But what astounded me the most was that someone would come and tell me, face to face. Once I became a local pastor, I had dozens of people who were ready to tell me when I blew it. But most people are not so privileged. At that time, I was an itinerant preacher, so nobody took me on. But this man did, and he is a precious friend.

He had read me right. I didn't appear to be angry, but I was! At the time, I was angry and frustrated because I traveled around as an itinerant preacher, trying to get Christians to evangelize and they weren't about to go out and do it. So my speaking seemed to be a kind of entertainment. I used to sing and play guitar, so I came as preacher, singer, and musician. And I got more and more angry as I saw people who were just looking for amusement. I was angry that my itinerant preaching wasn't producing what I thought it ought to produce.

But I had to learn that preaching or teaching isn't the only agent that produces the results of Christian obedience and maturity for which I was looking. The most important ingredient is fellowship—others to hold us accountable, and not just by sipping tea and patting one another on the back after church on Sunday morning. If you don't have some person or group in your life that will hold you accountable, your maturation process is going to be thwarted. So, if you don't already have such a person, find somebody! If you're not in such a group, find one you can join.

Tips for Giving and Receiving Encouragement

Once you have found an "Encourager," put these helpful ideas to work to strengthen one another.

- Decide if you would like to meet every two weeks or a minimum of once a month. An Encourager needn't be a spiritual giant, but someone who will challenge you. It should be someone of your same sex, with whom you feel comfortable.
- Pray together about choosing another Christian to join with you. Three people (maximum four) is ideal because if one person can't make a meeting, the other two can still meet.
- Set a time and place to meet regularly for one hour. This should be a place where you have a little privacy—perhaps an office, a living room, a quiet restaurant, etc. If your work schedule is inflexible, try lunch hours, evenings, or Sunday afternoon or evening.
- Each person should set several goals in each of these areas—Personal Spiritual Growth, Family, and Personal Ministry—and write them down. The following is a sample goal sheet that you can fill in (or use an index card to make your own).

My Spiritual Goals

I, _____, covenant with
God's help to allow him to mature me by being faithful in
meeting the following spiritual goals for my life.

Personal Growth	*Family*	*Personal Ministry*
_____	_____	_____
_____	_____	_____
_____	_____	_____
_____	_____	_____
_____	_____	_____
_____	_____	_____
_____	_____	_____
_____	_____	_____
_____	_____	_____

Signed: _____ *Date:* _____

You might want to follow this format in your "Encourager Group":

- Begin with a brief time of prayer.
- Give each person a written copy of your goals for the next month. Goals which are not met by the date you targeted should be reevaluated. Set a new date. Don't be too easy on each other or your growth will be slowed.
- Allot fifteen minutes per person for sharing your progress on meeting your goals. Share struggles and triumphs. Be honest with each other and ask for help or advice. Share special prayer needs.
- End with a time of prayer for each other, praying especially for unreached goals.
- End on time. Rotate leadership monthly. Keep things on schedule and away from discussion of other things.

These tips available from "Personal Renewal Month," a program from The John Guest Evangelistic Team, 3366 Burton St. S.E., Grand Rapids, MI 49546.

About every three months, analyze together what progress has been made and be honest with each other if you are not growing or if you feel your partner has not been faithful to his/her goals. One goal each person should eventually have is to begin an "Encourager Group" with two new people. This will allow each person to multiply spiritually and not get stale. Do not stop meeting until each person in your group has begun a new group.

New Vision

So what is koinonia? It's an expression of a new life in Christ, and it springs from fellowship with the Father and from the indwelling power of God's Spirit. Koinonia brings a whole new vision for our lives.

All the outgrowths of koinonia fellowship we've discussed thus far are not just for your own growth so that you can be personally pleased with yourself in a narcissistic way. We don't grow for growth's sake. We don't mature just so we can be mature Christians, admired by everybody else. The whole concept of growth and maturity comes within the context of the *vision of God's kingdom*.

Does this phrase sound familiar? "Thy Kingdom come, Thy will be done, on earth as it is in heaven." Christians need to grow because of the task we are called to do together. Let me emphasize that we are called to this task *together*—it's not just your personal calling, it is not mine alone. This is the *metoche* aspect of fellowship, when people are in joint participation, working toward a common goal.

We Are Called

Philippians 4 begins with these words: "Therefore, my brethren, whom I love and long for, my joy and crown, stand firm thus in the Lord, my beloved" (v. 1). Then he goes on to the real problem:

> I entreat Euodia and I entreat Syntyche to agree in the Lord. And I ask you also, true yokefellow, help these women, for they have labored side by side with me in the gospel together with Clement and the rest of my fellow workers, whose names are in the book of life. (Phil. 4:2–3)

Now I don't want to focus on Euodia and Syntyche being at odds with each other. And I don't want to emphasize Paul's calling them to account or his writing to this true yokefellow and calling *him* to account. The phrase I want to focus on is that Paul calls all of them "fellow laborers" or "co-workers in the gospel." Euodia, Syntyche, and Clement were in a working fellowship. They were co-laborers in the gospel. Their fellowship did not turn in on itself, for themselves. Rather, their fellowship was turned outward in a task. They dreamed together of making the kingdoms of this world the kingdom of God.

In Westminster Abbey, where all the sovereigns of England have been crowned for centuries, there is an inscription across the ceiling right over the spot where the kings and queens are crowned: "The kingdoms of this world have become the kingdom of our God." That statement is true prophetically, if you look down the corridors of time to an end result—we *are* in that process of making the kingdoms of this world the kingdom of our God.

If you are not heavily committed as co-laborers in the work of the gospel, if you do not have koinonia fellowship with others in a task-oriented ministry of making the kingdoms of this world the kingdom of our Lord and God, then you have missed a crucial opportunity to mature in Christ!

A Practical Faith

One of the great opportunities to mature as a follower of Christ is putting what you have learned to work. For example, you may mature a little bit in learning how to share your faith; you will mature by leaps and bounds in going out to do it. In fact, you will mature faster by *actually sharing* your faith than you will by learning six different methods for how to share your faith.

We Must Be United

Of course, the task of extending the kingdom of God cannot be achieved in isolation. I saw a film about Williamsburg, Virginia when I visited there. In the movie, Patrick Henry describes how the colonies on this North American continent had to bond together. Otherwise, George the Third and his troops could easily pick them off one at a time if each colony stood alone.

Christians in isolation are a sitting target for the world, the flesh, and the devil. They are easily picked off. But in task-oriented fellowship together, with the unified goal of making the kingdoms of the world the kingdom of God, we are going to mature at a tremendous pace.

A Heart for the Needy

Similarly, pastors struggle with standing alone in their counseling ministries. The world is incredibly needy! When you surface as someone people can call on to talk to or pray with, you will be deluged with needs and hurting people. A pastor needs fellowship that holds him accountable. Now, this is *not* a person to whom he indiscreetly passes on all the information he receives during a counseling session with another person! But it should be someone who also has a heart for people and a commitment to minister to them, someone who will pray for and support the counseling pastor.

You probably recognize this experience. We shy away from appearing able and willing to take on the hurts and burdens of needy people. We're afraid of the deluge, of getting dumped on. But you need to be part of a community of people who encourage and pray for you in that work of the gospel.

My closest friends are not those with whom I have sung lovely songs that have moved me emotionally. My closest fellowship is not with those at whose feet I have sat, being edified by their teaching. My closest fellowship is not with those who have been a part of the same church family at large in some sort of anonymity. My *real* fellowship is with those to whom, in harness together, there has been a commitment to work at getting something significant done for Jesus Christ.

A Call to Commitment

If you desire to mature in your character, then commit yourself with other people to the cause of Christ. You will actually become closer to them in a way that even counseling does not provide. This intimate friendship takes place because you are both given to the *cause* of making Jesus Christ known. That *metoche* fellowship draws you closer together and has a tremendous impact in terms of maturing you in Jesus Christ.

The Spirit of Fellowship

In John 17, Jesus prays that our fellowship will become so committed, loving, and active that the world will know by this phenomenon that he, Jesus, is really from God.

> I do not pray for these [the disciples] only, but also for those who believe in me through their word, that they may all be one; even as thou, Father, art in me, and I in thee, that they may also be in us, so that the world may believe that thou hast sent me. The glory which thou hast given me I have given to them, that they may be one even as we are one, I in them and thou in me, that they may become perfectly one, so that the world may know that thou hast sent me and hast loved them even as thou hast loved me. (John 17:20–23)

Jesus prays that we might be *one* (in fellowship) so that the world might know that he came from God. Christian fellowship is so antithetical to the character and nature of the world that when we enter into it genuinely, it amazes the world around us!

A church that really fellowships is obvious to the casual observer. Visitors are amazed at the closeness of the people in the congregation. Now, the closeness they feel may not be quite the way they perceive it, unless it is a very small church (and such a church would not stay small long; people are going to be attracted to it). But the reason the people in that church exude warmth and friendship is that they have participated in smaller group fellowship regularly: they have come together to discuss or do ministry; they have a regular Bible study; they are giving or receiving counseling; they come together for prayer; they are in the music program of the church, or the Sunday school ministry, or the Christian Education committee. In any number of different ways, the members of that congregation are plugged into fellowship. So, the visitor perceives a very large number of people who are close to each other when, in reality, all those people don't necessarily know all of the others.

Such a sense of warmth and love cannot be achieved when people gather together in larger worship unless they have been together in small group fellowship. You only have to know a dozen or fifteen people closely to feel as if you are part of that body of believers and part of what God is doing there. You don't have to be in on every ministry to feel you are participating in every ministry.

But be committed to that co-laboring in the work of the gospel, that fellowship of vulnerability in sharing what's going on in your lives, that fellowship of accountability. Gathering as a small group gives people the vision that this church really is a one-heart, one-mind, and one-spirit group. It is so contrary to the way of the world, where people are divisive, divided, scattered, schizophrenic, split all over the place, that people will notice!

People who are ready to criticize rather than to build up are transformed when they come in to worship and see the congregation of Jesus Christ at worship. They become convinced that Jesus really is the Lord!

The result of changed lives cannot be produced just by having a good choir or a great preacher. It springs from the fellowshiping circle of believers. Visitors to your church are not intimately aware of your fellowship. Obviously, to get in on that fellowship they've got to become a part of it.

But when they see people who have been in koinonia fellowship assembling for worship, they see the spirit of unity, the spirit of vulnerability, the spirit of accountability, and commitment to a common vision. Those are powerful tools for introducing them to Christ.

But you can't produce the warmth of koinonia in a large crowd unless it has been experienced in a small place with a smaller number.

Peter and his friends were faced with quite a discipleship dilemma! Three thousand people were converted on that first day. You can't teach 3,000 people at once. You can't disciple 3,000 people at once. But once they devoted themselves to koinonia fellowship, it became their discipling process. When they assembled, while they probably didn't know more than a few of the whole group of 3,000, there was probably a great sense of unity and community as they worshipped the Lord Jesus.

Koinonia fellowship is the primary means that God has given to us within the body of Jesus Christ, the family of God, by which we can grow. If you don't get in on that fellowship, your growth will be retarded. But if you do become a "Koinonia person," you'll move along and mature in Christ—at a rate that will surprise you and delight the Lord.

8

Six: Practice Giving

....

Each one must do as he has made up his mind,
not reluctantly or under compulsion, for God
loves a cheerful giver.

(2 Cor. 9:7)

There was a day when I used to believe that if someone gave his heart to Christ, the Lord automatically received his checkbook as well. In other words, as a pastor, all I had to do was preach about the love of God and draw people to put their faith in Christ. Then they, in turn, would give generously and happily to God and his work, and the ministry would grow and prosper.

Well, that "ain't necessarily so!" While what I have said is true of some, it is not true of the majority. It's been a hard awakening. In writing about what I believe the Bible teaches on giving to God, the Lord has thoroughly enriched me. As you read carefully, I expect that the Lord Jesus will similarly enrich you. There can be no significant Christian growth without the money we have at our disposal being placed in the Lord's hands for his use.

Three Primary Principles

God created and gave everything in the first place

The apostle Paul said, "What have you that you did not receive? If then you received it, why do you boast as if it were not a gift?" (1 Cor. 4:7). The mood and spirit of our age militate against this first and most powerful principle. Secular humanism places humanity at the center of the stage. In this scheme of things, man is the measure of all things; there is no external standard by which humankind is directed. Man is the focus in all things; there is no vision for anything beyond the human scene. Man is the possessor of all things; there is no one else to own it.

Our present generation has been called the "Me" generation. And why not, given the predominant philosophy of life? Advertisers urge us to spend extravagantly on ourselves because "I'm worth it" or because "I'm the most important person in my life—I owe it to myself." The climate of Western civilization has degenerated into a narcissistic self-love.

The Bible's teaching and the Christian faith stand in stark contrast to secular humanism. First of all, we owe everything to God and not to ourselves. The very life we live, God created. The air we take for granted, the minds which dream up bright ideas, the hands which produce and make things, the love of husband and wife, and the gift of children—all these things come from God. They are all God's ideas. He created them all. We are simply the recipients of all his goodness. Even what we have been able to produce by intelligence and hard work we have only developed from what God had already given us.

Now let me ask you this: Have you ever given something to a family member and then had them refuse to share it with you? One of the things that disturbs all parents is the possessiveness and selfishness of their children. You buy them a chocolate bar and they won't let you have one bite.

On the other hand, when your children share willingly, or even volunteer, and offer back to you without you making a request, isn't it a beautiful experience? Aren't you thrilled with them? God loves a cheerful giver. Second Corinthians 9:7 tells us that our giving should not be done grudgingly or of necessity. Is it not reasonable to suppose that you would want to share joyfully and gratefully with someone who has given you everything in the first place?

God has redeemed and adopted us

Just as the first principle demonstrates God's love in general by creating the world and all that is in it, the second principle demonstrates God's love for us in particular. God did not just hand things over to us and say, "Get on with it." As the apostle Paul said,

> While we were still weak, at the right time Christ died for the ungodly. Why, one will hardly die for a righteous man—though perhaps for a good man one will dare even to die. But God shows his love for us in that while we were yet sinners Christ died for us. (Rom. 5:6–8)

Jesus put it this way, "Greater love has no man than this, that a man lay down his life for his friends" (John 15:13).

It is almost inconceivable that when one is loved to this extent, he would want to withhold anything from the one who loves him. There are people who have done so much for me that there is virtually nothing I would not do for them. None, however, has done for me what the Lord Jesus has done. And none has given to me anything in comparison to what he has given.

The Lord did not do something "once upon a time" which we could easily forget. "For if while we were enemies we were reconciled to God by the death of his Son, much more, now that we are reconciled, shall we be saved by his life" (Rom. 5:10). We have an ongoing relationship with the living Christ. Just as a child is dependent on parents after birth, so we live our Christian lives close to the Lord Jesus and are dependent on him.

However, we never become independent of the Lord, as we do our human families. "In him we live and move and have our being," Acts 17:28 says. We walk with him and talk with him. A day never goes by that we don't self-consciously look to him in one way or another.

There is so much that redemption has brought to us. We no longer live for ourselves; we live for the One who has bought us. This is the new vision that the Christian has for his or her life. The joy and creativity which flow from this truth when we give ourselves to living it are beyond reckoning. Living for one's self becomes very boring and degenerating. Living for Jesus Christ and his kingdom is challenging and invigorating. You never retire, and you're never put out to pasture.

The Church has been given the most important task

The most important task of the church is "to proclaim the gospel to a lost world." Here I speak of the church both as an institution organized on a street corner, and as the multinational influence it is, person by person, in its millions of members. But I venture to say that it is only as the church on the street corner does its job that the church members out in the secular and strife-torn world will be effective.

Enough emphasis cannot be placed on this aspect of the church's task in our modern world. It is the "equipping of the saints for the work of ministry." This is an extremely crucial process—especially in our contemporary world. Our young people grow up under pressures which we adults can barely conceive. Whether it is movies, magazines, music, or television, our young people are bombarded with anti-Christian values. And as if that's not enough, the American Civil Liberties Union falls over backward to "protect" our young people from any overt Christian influence in their education.

Today, in the wake of family and moral disintegration, you will find a growing emphasis on a Christian education for young people. The market is flooded with Christian family literature, and churches build family life development into their education (such as premarital counseling and ministry to singles and the divorced). There was a day when hardly anyone ever sought counseling. Today the church that cares is deluged, and pastors are overwhelmed with counseling needs. Much more is being expected of the institutional church than at any time in recent history.

To equip Christians for the work of ministry will take more than the proverbial "one man and his dog who went to mow a meadow." Experience has shown that the more laity you train, the more professional staff you need to keep up with the work that the lay ministries create. Somewhere along the way, perhaps because the United States is embarrassed by its wealth, the notion became commonly expressed that the American church ought not to spend so much money on itself.

There is a ring of genuine piety and altruism about this statement that resonates in the Christian's heart. The last thing we want to do is "spend money on ourselves." But the question that must be asked is simply this, "Does the church really want to take on the secular world?" Do the various needs of the world that we have described demand specialized training? And when the ministries are developed, do they need pastoring and monitoring for continued growth and encouragement? I think the issue is not whether we are spending money on ourselves, but whether we are investing wisely in the work of the gospel and enlarging and strengthening the kingdom of God. The church is not a charity; it's a mission station with a God-given task to get on with. Let's stop measuring what we give away against what we keep, and start asking the question, "Where is the investment of that money going to do the most for the kingdom of God?"

The question of financial distribution would virtually disappear if Christians tithed 10 percent of their income to the work of the gospel. God has called us to the magnificent task of proclaiming the unsearchable riches of Christ. Do you believe that? If the church doesn't do it, who will?

I once asked a very successful businessman, who was a Christian and the chief executive officer of a multinational corporation, "If the church had been doing the job God called it to do, would the world be in its present state of affairs?" His answer was a vehement "No!"

Let's stop wringing our hands and deploring past failures and get on with what God has called us to do.

How Much?

That Christians should be "givers" is never in question. How much *is*. Interestingly, when someone asks, "How much?" they are rarely asking, "How much do you need?" Usually it is, "How little can I give?" Again, this talk of real money and actual amounts forces us to realize how tight-fisted we are. The humanness in us always wants to hoard. If we don't need to spend money on ourselves now, we know we will in the near future. The Bible pictures a man who built bigger barns to hold onto everything he could (Luke 12:18). We know what was in that man's heart. It's in ours.

Old Testament Giving

Under the Old Covenant (before Jesus came), the tithe formed the basis for giving to God. The tithe was 10 percent off the top. This concept is pervasive throughout the

Old Testament: in Genesis 14:20, Abraham gave a tithe to Melchizedek, and in Genesis 28:22, Jacob vowed to give God a tithe of all he might possess. But here's the classic passage from the prophet Malachi:

> Will man rob God? Yet you are robbing me. But you say, "How are we robbing thee?" In your tithes and offerings . . . Bring the full tithes into the storehouse . . . and thereby put me to the test, says the LORD of hosts. (Mal. 3:8, 10)

Although the tithe was the basis of giving for the Old Testament believer, there were other kinds of offerings which demonstrated that God had first claim on everything. For instance, the firstborn of oxen and sheep were to be offered to God (Exod. 22:30). All the firstfruits of the land were to be offered to the Lord (2 Chron. 31:5).

Above and beyond the tithe or the firstfruit was the *voluntary* offering. The nature of this response to God goes beyond *obligation* to the human need to express heartfelt gratitude. When things go well, what do we do? We all know the experience of being overwhelmed with joy. There are times when ecstasy and gratitude well up inside and nearly choke us. We can't wait to tell someone about a new job, a promotion, the birth of a son or granddaughter, or the coming to faith of a relative. Just as God has given us the human emotion of thankfulness, so he provided for those early believers an appropriate spiritual response—the freewill or thank offering (Lev. 7:12, 16).

So, under the old arrangement of the law, the tithe and the firstfruits represented God's claim, and the thank offering and freewill offering represented the people's gratitude. This system of giving provided for the worship of God and the welfare of the people. It demonstrated the need to love the Lord with all your heart, and your neighbor as yourself. It was highly religious, but extremely practical. It was both very specific and beautifully spontaneous.

New Testament Giving

The new covenant of Jesus Christ is not a covenant of *law*, but of *grace*. The Christian faith, therefore, is not expressed in adhering to religious regulations, but in terms of showing compelling love. Zacchaeus gave away half of all he possessed (Luke 19:8). Barnabas sold his land and gave all the proceeds (Acts 4:37). The churches of Macedonia gave "according to their means" and even "beyond their means" (2 Cor. 8:3).

Being poor was not used as an excuse for not giving. There was no sense in which those who were poor left it up to those who were rich. It was simply that those who had more gave more. In addition, some had the "gift" of giving. Among the gifts listed for ministry in Romans 12:8, note these words: "He who contributes" is to do so "in liberality" or in "simplicity" (KJV). People who have this gift of ministry do not necessarily have great wealth, but they have great generosity. They lift us all to a greater awareness of our need to be joyous and generous givers.

The tithe for Christians is the bare minimum. It's a beginning place, based on the expectations God had placed on those of another age and dispensation. If the requirement was ten percent in the Old Testament (*before* Christ's sacrifice for us), how can we, who know ourselves to be purchased with a great price, give anything less?

The spirit of genuine Christian giving is much more in accord with the spirit of the thank offering or the free will offering. It's a response to "the deep, deep love of Jesus," as one hymn writer has put it. C. T. Studd, an English missionary who went first to China, then India, and then Africa, carried as his life motto: "If Christ be God and died for me, then no sacrifice I can make for him will ever be too great."

Thirteen Reasons Not to Tithe

"Will man rob God?" Malachi 3:8 says. When we withhold from God what both he and we know is rightly his, we are robbing God. Satan loves for you to do that. One thing you can count on is that in this piece of spiritual warfare, Satan is on your side. He will feed you every excuse imaginable for you to keep on robbing God. For not only does he want you on his satanic team, but he also wants the sharing of the gospel to be pathetic; the life of the church to be pitiful; for Christians to spend their money on anything but the gospel ministry so that the church is constantly fussing about the shortage of money rather than the advance of the gospel.

Here are thirteen excuses Satan has been known to suggest and then affirm, so that you should rob God:

Maybe next year. I can't afford it now!

Have you ever said that? How about last year? The year before? Five or ten years ago? You may have used this one for years. The King of Procrastination says, "Always put off to next year what you could do this year."

Other people earn more than I do.

"It's much easier to tithe from $50,000 than it is from $10,000. Since others have so much more than I do, let them carry the load. They can afford it!"

If you have already established the first excuse, the second one follows it nicely. We all know someone who makes much more money than we do. But let me ask you, Do you remember your first job that earned you $4,700 a year? Now, of course, you are earning much more than that. But do you have more discretionary money—money that is not spoken for, that you could give without missing it? Of course you don't. Some of you still struggle to pay your bills with $40,000–$75,000 a year. Those in the $15,000 bracket wonder why. But we all know the answer. As you earn more, you spend more. The King of Greed says, "Keep it up."

When I finish my payments, I'll be able to give more.

"When I finish my car payments, or my mortgage payments, or the payments for my children's tuition, then I'll have a bit more money and I'll be able to give more." Then you make the payments for whatever it is you are buying. But a strange thing happens: as you near the end of your payments, you begin to dream of something else you'd like to buy.

When my children are grown, I'll be able to give more.

This is a perfectly reasonable excuse for those of you with young families. But do you know what happens when the children are grown? Then people say, "Now that we've put the kids through school, and they are on their own, we need to look after ourselves. We've done our share. We'll leave it up to the younger folks." It's a catch-22. When you are young, older folks are better off; when you are old, younger folks are better off. You are never the right age to give generously.

When business picks up, or when I get a raise, I'll give more.

This is a great excuse when the economy is depressed. But have you ever noticed that business never seems to pick up? We may climb out of a hole, but we never come to the point where business is so great that we have plenty to give. If we get that raise, it never quite covers inflation or our new expenses or our new tax bracket. So we continue to feel justified in skimping on our giving.

I do not agree with everything that is going on in the church.

I guarantee that each of you could fill a legal-size sheet with things in the church with which you disagree. But in which area of your life is everything just the way you want it to be? Is that true in your marriage? Your home? With your friends? With your children? At work? In your community? In your political party? The truth is that Murphy's Law applies to every area of our lives. Things are never exactly the way we think they should be. And Satan is committed to keeping Christians fussing among themselves.

This is a rich church. They don't need my money.

Well, there may be some rich people in every church, but it does not mean it's a rich church. Every church struggles constantly to meet the needs of its people in a complex society. Men and women with tremendous responsibilities in specialized ministries need to be supported in their tasks.

I pay taxes, and I give to other things.

I'm sure that is true. But God's people need to give their money to God's work as a first priority. Do you know that most corporations have policies which inhibit their giving to religious work? So do most charitable foundations. Even Christian foundations are generally directed to support paraministries (ministries outside of the church). If Christians do not make their church a priority, then there is no other source.

Compared with other churches, this one does fine.

That may be true. But how well are those other churches doing? Do you realize that ninety percent of all clergy are on the verge of collapse? Not only do they administer a church, but they also run the youth ministry, prepare young couples for marriage and families for baptism, comfort the sick and bereaved, bury the dead, conduct worship services, and teach Bible studies. They may even type the church bulletin. Is that a fair standard of comparison for the ministry God would have us accomplish? Do you take what is mediocre, or even desperate, and make it the measure?

God does not expect us to tithe in this day and age.

In other words, tithing was great for the Jews and early Christians, but we have many more responsibilities and expenses. Therefore, God does not expect us to tithe. Of course that sounds reasonable, but it is really ridiculous when you realize that we are the wealthiest people who have ever lived. We are in the top half of the top one percent of the whole of humanity for all time!

I give in other ways—my time, my energy, and my talent.

That is phenomenal. But while it is terrific that you give your time, your energy, and your talent, they can never make up for the commitment God requires of your money. We need to give both.

This is a bad year.

Do you know that each year we have increased the budget, and that each year we have been told that this is a bad year to do that? It is no different this year; it will be no different next year. The newsmakers love bad news. And more than anything else, Satan loves bad news.

When I become a wage earner, I will tithe.

This, of course, is an excuse for young people. Do you know that it is because the older folks used this excuse when they were young that we have the preceding twelve excuses? Now is the time to begin to tithe. If you begin while your income is small, as your income grows, tithing will be easier because the other nine-tenths will be growing as well. The habit will be formed and the right attitude developed.

Because the Christian church of today uses these excuses, it is crawling when it ought to be sprinting. And Satan loves to have it so.

Let's Get Practical

Purposeful planning

Generous giving demands purposeful planning. "Each one must do as he has made up his mind, not reluctantly or under compulsion, for God loves a cheerful giver" (2 Cor. 9:7). The clear implication of these words is that prior thought must go into Christian giving. Each one is to make up his mind. We must take time to think through what appropriate giving is for us.

Since we are encouraged to avoid "reluctance or compulsion," pray first. Perhaps the following will express what you want to pray. If it's to be a family discussion, have a family member lead you, or pray for you all, as you feel most comfortable.

Dear heavenly Father,
Everything I have, you gave me. Your Son died for me. All that I hope for in the future is in your gracious hands. I brought nothing into this world, and I will carry nothing out. Between now and when I see you face to face, make me a good manager of all you have given to me. Help me now to think through, in your presence, how I spend the money you have given me. Help me to plan what I should give to your work. Help me to be generous. Help me to pledge joyfully. Make this a holy time for me (and my family) as I deal with

this practical but sensitive business of giving. I pray in the name of Jesus Christ, my Lord. Amen.

One of the keys to cheerful giving is making up your mind ahead of time. If you have to struggle with how much you give, every time you give, experience proves that not only do you give meagerly, but there is no pleasure in it either.

Be systematic

An important part of planning is to give systematically. Some of you are paid weekly, others every other week, and for some it's once a month. But however it may be, let the first check you write be your gift to the work of God. Not only can you offer it as a firstfruit, but more importantly, you acknowledge afresh each time your gratitude that "All things come of thee, O Lord, and of thine own have we given thee!"

Pledging

Pledging encourages three important spiritual exercises. The first comes in the process of planning what you will give—you have to *determine your priorities.* How you spend your money is one of the things that determines what you count important in life. Too many miss this spiritual experience through lack of planning.

The second spiritual exercise pledging calls for is *faith.* Many don't pledge because they are uncertain about their earnings and their future. Others think it presumptuous to pledge. Well, if your economic circumstances change—downward or upward—you can always review your pledge. But one of the essential ingredients of the Christian is walking by faith (2 Cor. 5:7), and pledging is a practical exercise which can encourage such faith.

The third spiritual exercise that comes with pledging is *commitment.* Too many miss the joy and fulfillment that comes from making a commitment. We live in an age of noncommittal "Let's see what tomorrow will bring." One of the unique experiences of the human personality is the ability to make self-conscious personal commitments. God has made the choice to serve him a spiritual experience. Pledging to his work is a very practical way to enter into this spiritual experience.

Pledging also helps the leadership of the church to plan ahead for its ministry. Granted, you may say, "Why doesn't the church leadership walk by faith in its planning and trust the Lord to bring in what the church needs?" This is a valid question, and to tell you the truth, there are churches and ministries which have organized themselves according to this principle—some with notable success.

But the answer we give is really a balance of the two positions. You can put your faith to work in pledging, as a spiritual exercise, and the church leadership can put its faith to work in two ways: by joining you in your faith that God will provide what you have pledged, and by going ahead with the ministry it believes the Lord is calling the church to fulfill (which means going beyond the church budget that is known). This is "faith budgeting"—faith that the Lord will provide and bless the ministry accordingly. This dual faith elicits the strengths of both positions.

Teaching children to give

"Train up a child in the way he should go, and when he is old he will not depart from it" (Prov. 22:6). Perhaps the reason so few adults give as they should goes back to their childhood training. When you give a tithe of a dollar, it's only ten cents. It doesn't look like much. But when your child grows and his income grows, the habit and attitude of tithing should grow as well. Then when he arrives in the 50 percent tax bracket, tithing to the work of God is no shock to his system.

My recommendation is that those of you who are parents teach your children the principles of tithing. As soon as they are old enough to understand, they should make a pledge and begin to put their pennies aside in a jar or cup. One young lady described how when she was a child, she had three baby-food jars. One was labeled savings, one church, and the other spending. When she got her dollar allowance, she would put a dime in "savings," a dime in "church," and eighty cents in "spending." Your children would never forget that image.

What about high school and college students?

If young people are serious about their Christian faith, they should give to God. The pressure on adolescents to be "self-centered" is enormous—they have to have the "right" clothes, go to the "right" places, buy the "right" records, have the "right" hairstyle, etc. It all costs a small fortune.

This is the most critical time for you to give to the work of God. Take time out from wondering what to buy next and pray about your giving to God. Then pledge and see it through.

Where should I give?

Normally your tithe should be given to your home church, if it's the center of spiritual nourishment and encouragement for you and your family. If it's the place to which you bring friends so that they might find Christ, then it's where your tithe belongs. If it's the place you want to send friends because their marriage is in trouble or their children are in trouble, then it's where your tithe belongs. Otherwise, when you are thinking seriously about marriage, who will do the premarital counseling? Or who will visit you when you are in the hospital? Or support and encourage you when you lose your job?

Once you become a serious-minded Christian, there are so many claims on your giving from other valid Christian ministries. You may be struggling with this right now. What should you do? Here are two answers:

1. When a church family brings its tithes into its own church, then that church has significant resources to distribute in missions and other ministries. A local church needs to take its own missionary task seriously before it can take on a larger missionary cause in a significant way. Most important, we must realize that we are all parts of one great task—spreading the gospel throughout the world.

2. The tithe is the beginning place for Christian giving. When the Lord sets our hearts free to give to him as he has given to us, there is always the overabundance of our gratitude which is represented in thank offerings and free will offerings. The sooner the church becomes serious about tithing, the sooner it will move to beyond the tithe. And the sooner Christians get the tithe in their own barn, the sooner we can move from theoretical discussions about its distribution to the real work of taking on the world in a way we have never been able to before.

Some of us may need to take a practical step toward tithing. Given present circumstances in your family economics, it may not appear feasible to tithe immediately. But set yourself on the course of being there in three years.

It may be that you are "not there" spiritually. Well, do the same thing. Move toward the tithe and pray that God will move you spiritually as well. Do the necessary things to grow spiritually. Make the necessary changes in your heart's attitude and in your thinking. Jesus said, "Where your treasure is, there will your heart be also" (Luke 12:34). If you want to grow spiritually, take the Lord at his word and get more of "your treasure" into his kingdom and its work. See if your heart doesn't follow!

Some healthy examples

There is a right way to let people know what is happening in the rest of the Christian world so that we can be challenged to a new perspective. And this can happen through churches just like yours.

For instance, I spent time in Modesto, California at the First Baptist Church. Modesto is not an enormous or wealthy city—it epitomizes American suburbia. But do you know what? The total budget of that church in 1983 was $2.858 million, of which $800,000 was capital development. Their average Sunday morning attendance was 2,058. In 1988 their total budget was $4.2 million.

Truro Parish Church is in Fairfax, Virginia, a Washington, D. C. suburb. Property is very expensive there, and the population extremely mobile. Truro's budget for 1983 was $1.2 million in operation and $600,000 in capital giving—a total of $1.8 million. By 1988 their budget had grown to $2.986 million!

I use these two churches as examples because neither is in the "super church" category. They do not have national television outreaches, like Dr. Robert Schuller's Crystal Cathedral. They are thriving churches in communities that have their own particular problems, just like yours does. "The point is this: he who sows sparingly will also reap sparingly, and he who sows bountifully will also reap bountifully" (2 Cor. 9:6). When the people of God give to the work of God, there is an outpouring of the blessing of God.

The Blessing of Giving to God

We have discussed fairly thoroughly the reasons for giving to God. This last truth needs to be carefully presented and spiritually perceived. I have heard preachers pander to the greed and selfishness of their audience. They make "what you are going to get back" the major reason for giving. It grieves me that they have taken a truth from God's

Word and so abused it that they stimulate greed rather than graciousness.

Giving to God is not primarily an obligation but a blessing. The man who is so taken up with himself and—for fear of losing his dignity or being taken advantage of—clings to himself becomes a loser. The opposite alternative is the truth we are after. The more people give of themselves, the more they are willing to be used, and the more significant and satisfied they become. Luke quotes Jesus as saying, "It is more blessed to give than to receive" (Acts 20:35). And in Luke 6:38, Jesus says, "Give, and it will be given to you; good measure, pressed down, shaken together, running over, will be put into your lap. For the measure you give will be the measure you get back."

You sometimes hear it expressed like this, "You get out of it no more than you put in." That's the way it is. God doesn't want to deprive us. He is constantly gracious; he wants to bless us. But we are headed in the opposite direction, fooled by the lies of advertisers and our own selfish appetites.

The word "blessed" really means a "deep-seated joy." Modern translations sometimes use the word "happy." But the Bible is talking about something deeper than a whimsical mood of the moment. Read again these words:

> Bring the full tithes into the storehouse, that there may be food in my house; and thereby put me to the test, says the LORD of hosts, if I will not open the windows of heaven for you and pour down for you an overflowing blessing. (Mal. 3:10)

Are you prepared to believe that by faith? If we bring the full tithe to the ministry of God, God will be gracious to us. He will pour out his blessings from heaven in such measure they will overflow. One of the reasons we have all the earlier excuses is that we have not received all the blessings

God wants to give us. Our hands have been closed, grasping onto what we have. God cannot pour out his blessings into tight fists. As you open your hands and make your resources available to God's work, you will receive all the blessings God longs to give you.

When I was a lad in England, we were poor. One of my recurring dreams was of wandering along my favorite stream and discovering lots of money in the grass alongside it. After looking around carefully to be sure no one was watching, I would get on my knees and begin to gather up that money. And the more I would gather and stuff into my pockets, the more there was still in the grass. My chief worry became, *I won't be able to get it all!*

In the same way, God wants to bless us, to give us so much that we do not have enough space in which to contain it. But until we open our hands and give to the ministry of Jesus Christ and his gospel, we will always find ourselves lacking. When we do give with open hands, God will be faithful and will fulfill his promise to us.

Will you take God at his word? Will you pledge at least ten percent of your income to the work of Jesus Christ? God has promised that if you will do so, by the end of the year you will not be lacking.

Dear Heavenly Father,
Forgive us all our excuses. Forgive us that for so long we have had our hands closed so tight that we have been closed off from all that you would give to us and do for us. We pray that in many hearts there will be a new faith to trust you for tomorrow.
Encourage our faith according to your promises to us through Jesus Christ, our Lord. Amen.

9

Go for It!

I have fought the good fight, I have finished the
race, I have kept the faith. Henceforth there is
laid up for me the crown of righteousness, which
the Lord, the righteous judge, will award to me
on that Day, and not only to me but also to all
who have loved his appearing.

(2 Tim. 4:7–8)

The prison cell in which I stood that lovely spring afternoon was damp and cold. Outside the birds were singing
in the blossoming trees and the tempo of the traffic was beginning to pick up as the streets of Rome prepared for one
of their four daily rush hours. (The Italians take a two-hour
siesta, so everyone rushes home at two P.M. to return to
work later in the afternoon.)

The prison cell was an underground cave. A hole in the
roof, covered with bars, was a reminder of the harsh de-
spair that accompanied imprisonment, for prisoners were
dropped through that hole to languish until they died—except for a few who were retrieved for execution. This is
where two great heroes of the Christian faith spent their
last days on earth; the apostles Peter and Paul. Peter was
taken out and crucified upside down—at his own request
because he felt unworthy to die exactly like the Lord Jesus.

Paul, because he was a Roman citizen, was led from that damp, miserable cave to be beheaded.

As I stood there, using my imagination to fly back across the years, I remembered Peter, the young, strident fisherman called by Jesus to leave his nets and the idyllic Sea of Galilee to go fishing for men. It was Peter who wrote, "Always be prepared to make a defense to any one who calls you to account for the hope that is in you . . . " (1 Peter 3:15). He walked from that cell, ready to give such an account, even in his death.

Then I saw Paul, huddled against the wall, writing to Timothy, his young disciple to whom he gave the leadership of the church in Ephesus. Paul, aware that the end of his life was imminent, wrote to Timothy,

> For I am already on the point of being sacrificed; the time of my departure has come. I have fought the good fight, I have finished the race, I have kept the faith. Henceforth there is laid up for me the crown of righteousness, which the Lord, the righteous judge, will award to me on that Day, and not only to me but also to all who have loved his appearing. (2 Tim. 4:6–8)

When later I shared this prison experience with my congregation, I was moved to tears as I spoke of the great apostle, staring death in the face, summing up his life in such enthusiastic "go for it" terms. In effect, Paul was writing his epitaph—his personal estimation of how he had lived for the Lord Jesus.

What's Your Epitaph?

I have a friend who owns a granite quarry and sells memorials and tombstones. He shocked me on one occasion by trying to sell me my tombstone. I said, "Do people really do that while they are still living?"

"Yes!" he said. "They buy their burial lot, place the tomb-stone at the head of it, with their names (husband and wife) and etch in only the birth dates. After they have died, their death date is added."

I thought to myself, "If I were to do that, what epitaph would I write to sum up my life?" Most epitaphs are written by someone else about the deceased. But if you bought your own tombstone, you could write your own epitaph. Again I thought, "What would I want it to be?"

That's the question I'd like you to ask yourself as we come to the close of this book. If you, right now, could write an epitaph that would sum up your life as you hope to live it, what would it be? Of course, one incentive to have it be worthy of our Lord Jesus would be to consider what others might write about us—if they could be honest! Maybe it would be something like:

He was mediocre.
She was always timid.
Coward!
He took care of number one.
She could have been spectacular.
If only he had "gone for it!"

What would be an honest summation of your life as a Christian if today were the day of reckoning?

Running the Race

If you are anything like me, you want to go out with the flags flying high, the cannons blazing, and the trumpets blaring. Even those of you who are at the retirement end of your life know that God does not have retirement plans for you. He never writes you off as a has-been because you are a senior citizen. He would never instigate a Christian Association of Retired Persons, if that means suspending you from active Christian service.

Don't be tempted to squander ten or twenty years of your life living for yourself because the world around you tells you, "That's what you have worked for all these years!" God abolish the notion that we work hard all our lives so that we might spend a decade or two in idle pleasure-seeking! What a waste of our wonderful, God-given lives, assets, and opportunities. What a waste of the kingdom of God within us.

Take Paul's statement, "I have finished the race" (2 Tim. 4:7). Every distance runner knows that if he can cross the finish line with energy left over to burn, he has not run the race he should have run. Theoretically, there should be nothing left. All should be spent. That's how Paul understood the Christian life—"It's a race."

In recent years, Christians have taken to the concept (and I know it's biblical) of describing their lives as "their walk." Look at what Paul wrote to his church at Corinth:

> Do you not know that in a race all the runners compete, but only one receives the prize? So run that you may obtain it. Every athlete exercises self-control in all things . . . Well, I do not run aimlessly, I do not box as one beating the air; but I pommel my body and subdue it, lest after preaching to others I myself should be disqualified. (1 Cor. 9:24–27)

So run that you may obtain it. Don't be content to run in the middle of the pack! Run to win!

Toward the Finish Line

Don't misunderstand the apostle Paul. He's not suggesting mere competition, so that we try to beat one another out of first place. The emphasis is on *running as if to win;* giving the race all we've got. "So run" is where the action lies. The writer to the Hebrews captures the same imagery and sets the Christian in a great Olympian arena with myriads of spectators cheering from the grandstands of heaven (see Heb. 12:1–2).

To impel us to run, and to *keep on* running hard, we are given two incredible incentives. One I have already alluded to—the cheering crowds. Right at this moment, see that "cloud of witnesses" and hear the roar of their voices charging you to strain every muscle and pour out that last drop of energy. In the crowd are Peter, Paul, Augustine, Martin Luther, Thomas Cranmer, John Knox, D. L. Moody, Robert E. Lee, Billy Sunday, Jim Elliot, and Martin Luther King, Jr. Along with thousands upon thousands of others who have already run their races, they are now cheering you on. That's the first incentive.

The second is the finish line. It is Jesus. When we are exhorted to look to "Jesus the source and the goal of our faith" (Heb. 12:2 J. B. PHILLIPS), we are given the athlete's race-winning principle. "Don't look around at the rest of the field. Look at the finish line and throw yourself at it." For the believer, the Lord Jesus is the finish line. We set our eyes on him and throw ourselves into his arms.

What an incentive! You will often see athletes in competition fall into the arms of their trainers after they have crossed the finish line. Waiting there for you is the Lord Jesus. Can you imagine, having given all you have to give, falling into the outstretched and waiting arms of Jesus? Steve Green, a Christian singer, sings a song based on the account of the woman who came and poured out a full container of very expensive perfumed oil over Jesus (see Matt. 26:6–13). In using this incident, he sings of his own life being poured out and used up for Jesus, just like the perfume. Poured out and used up—that's what is involved in the Christian mind-set when we speak about "going for it!" It means we have no intention of crossing the finish line with unused resources in reserve!

George Whitefield is the preacher who is given credit for being God's primary instrument in what is known as the "Great Awakening" of the eighteenth century. When people would encourage him to slow down, he would say, "It is better to burn out than to rust out." Amen! The world awaits a new generation of Christians who will become all they can be for the Lord Jesus and his kingdom.

Go for It!

By the grace of God, you can be such a runner for Jesus. Will you write your epitaph today? Find a quiet place. On your knees, determine before the Lord that your life is going to count. In the face of all the adversaries (even some in the church) who are trying to pour you into the mold of mediocrity, pledge before the Lord that the story of your life will be "Go for it." And then *go for it!*

> I am no longer my own but Yours.
> Put me to what You will.
> Put me to doing.
> Put me to suffering.
> Let me be employed for You or laid aside for You.
> Let me be full, let me be empty.
> Let me have all things, let me have nothing.
> I freely and wholeheartedly yield all things to
> Your pleasure and disposal.
> And now glorious and blessed God,
> Father, Son and Holy Spirit
> You are mine and I am Yours.
> So be it. And this covenant now made
> On earth, let it be ratified in Heaven. Amen.

> John Wesley